# Children and the Internet:

## A Zen Guide for Parents and Educators

**Prentice Hall Series in Innovative Technology**

Dennis R. Allison, David J. Farber, and Bruce D. Shriver   *Series Advisors*

| | |
|---|---|
| **Bhasker** | *A VHDL Primer* |
| **Bhasker** | *VHDL Syntax* |
| **Blachman** | *Mathematica: A Practical Approach* |
| **Chan and Mourad** | *Digital Design Using Field Programmable Gate Arrays* |
| **El-Rewini, Lewis, and Ali** | *Task Scheduling in Parallel and Distributed Systems* |
| **Jenkins** | *Designing with FPGAs and CPLDs* |
| **Johnson** | *Superscalar Microprocessor Design* |
| **Kane and Heinrich** | *MIPS RISC Architecture, Second Edition* |
| **Kehoe and Mixon** | *Children and the Internet: A Zen Guide for Parents and Educators* |
| **Kehoe** | *Zen and the Art of the Internet, Fourth Edition* |
| **Lawson** | *Parallel Processing in Industrial Real-Time Applications* |
| **Nelson, ed.** | *Systems Programming with Modula-3* |
| **Nutt** | *Open Systems* |
| **Rose** | *The Internet Message: Closing the Book with Electronic Mail* |
| **Rose** | *The Little Black Book: A Practical Perspective on OSI Directory Services* |
| **Rose** | *The Open Book: A Practical Perspective on OSI* |
| **Rose** | *The Simple Book: An Introduction to Management of TCP/IP-Based Internets* |
| **Rose** | *The Simple Book: An Introduction to Networking Management* |
| **Shapiro** | *A C++ Toolkit* |
| **Slater** | *Microprocessor-Based Design* |
| **SPARC International, Inc.** | *The SPARC Architecture Manual, Version 8* |
| **SPARC International, Inc.** | *The SPARC Architecture Manual, Version 9* |
| **Steinmetz and Nahrstedt** | *Multimedia: Computing, Communications & Applications* |
| **Treseler** | *Designing State Machine Controllers Using Programmable Logic* |
| **Wirfs-Brock, Wilkerson, and Weiner** | *Designing Object-Oriented Software* |

# Children and the Internet:

## A Zen Guide for Parents and Educators

**Brendan P. Kehoe**
**Victoria Mixon**

To join a Prentice Hall PTR Internet mailing list,
point to: **http://www.prenhall.com/register**

**Prentice Hall PTR**
**Upper Saddle River, New Jersey 07458**
**http://www.prenhall.com**

**Library of Congress Cataloging-in-Publication Data**

Kehoe, Brendan P.

     Children and the Internet : a Zen guide for parents and educators
  / Brendan Kehoe, Victoria Mixon.

       p.  cm. -- (Innovative technology series)

     Includes bibliographical references and index.

     ISBN 0-13-244674-X

     1. Education--Computer network resources.  2. Internet (Computer
network) and children.  I. Mixon, Victoria. II. Title. III. Series

LB1044.87.K45   1996

025.06'37--dc20                        96-9693

                                            CIP

Editorial/production supervision: *Joanne Anzalone*
Manufacturing manager: *Alexis R. Heydt*
Acquisitions editor: *Karen Gettman*
Editorial assistant: *Barbara Alfieri*
Cover design: *Design Source*
Cover design director: *Jerry Votta*

 © 1997 Prentice Hall PTR
Prentice-Hall, Inc.
A Simon & Schuster Company
Upper Saddle River, New Jersey 07458

The publisher offers discounts on this book when ordered in bulk quantities.

For more information, contact:
Corporate Sales Department
Prentice Hall PTR
1 Lake Street
Upper Saddle River, NJ 07458

Phone: 800-382-3419, Fax: 201-236-7141
E-mail: `corpsales@prenhall.com`

Printed in the United States of America
10 9 8 7 6 5 4 3 2 1

# ISBN 0-13-244674-X

Prentice-Hall International (UK) Limited, *London*
Prentice-Hall of Australia Pty. Limited, *Sydney*
Prentice-Hall Canada Inc., *Toronto*
Prentice-Hall Hispanoamericana, S.A., *Mexico*
Prentice-Hall of India Private Limited, *New Delhi*
Prentice-Hall of Japan, Inc., *Tokyo*
Simon & Schuster Asia Pte. Ltd., *Singapore*
Editora Prentice-Hall do Brasil, Ltda., *Rio de Janeiro*

*Dedicated to our sweethearts:*
*Elana McCoy*
*and*
*Jeffrey Osier*

# Contents

# Preface

The offerings of the Internet are nearly boundless. No matter what your interests may be, the Net probably has something to at least whet your palate for more, if not provide you with all of the information you're seeking.

The popularity of the Internet started in a fairly exclusive area: technical engineers, scientists, and government agencies used it to keep in touch with each other and share their research. However, in recent years the usability of the Net has extended itself to be applicable to nearly anyone—no longer must you know the obscure points of a computer to truly take advantage of this global medium. Parents around the world are using the Net in their living rooms, and teachers are actively making the Internet a strong part of their curriculum.

While at first glance the Internet may seem to be easily used with its vast capabilities, these parents and teachers are confronted with a new challenge: learning to use it in a safe, productive setting. The simplicity of some of the Net's features, like the World Wide Web, may lead you to expect everything regarding its actual use to be that self-explanatory. Alas, there are a number of caveats that you should heed.

Using the Internet can be a very positive experience; you just need a solid foundation to take full advantage of it.

If you're in the field of K-12 education—whether you're an experienced teacher, a librarian, a school principal, or a parent supervising your children's studies—you've probably heard of *educational technology.* If you haven't, you soon will.

Since late 1995, when President Clinton announced NII, the Networked Information Infrastructure, schools across the country have been deluged with expectations that they, too, will step into Cyberspace. Everyone is bandying jargon about terminals, cable wires, modems, hook-ups, access, teleconferencing, video, and resources. Everyone, from parents to newscasters, is talking about the future of K-12 education on the Internet. Everyone is struggling to conceive of a classroom where information comes out of computer screens instead of textbooks.

Unlike anything in the history of modern education, computer savvy is taking schools by storm. You're riding the eye of a tornado. And what do you call this phenomenon? Educational technology.

Look at childrens' faces today while you're teaching them something new. You'll recognize the change in their eyes when it suddenly makes sense. Remember how it felt the first time you figured out why 1 + 1 = 2? The epiphany.

A lifetime after that first epiphany, you can look around and see how it changed everything about your world. You can see it in the classroom, when you're teaching the very first steps of a new lesson, knowing from your perspective how one moment of clarity blossoms into an entire field of knowledge and how that knowledge changes lives.

We hope that this book will make your trip into Cyberspace a positive one. In the coming chapters, you will read about the various issues you may encounter along the way—safety issues, drafting acceptable use policies for your school, and how much of the Net should be part of a classroom—as well as some possible starting points for your exploration.

As children enter the coming century, they will be faced with new challenges that their parents and teachers can't begin to imagine. What we can do today is give kids the knowledge and experience that will benefit them in the years to come.

So join us and thousands of others like you in the epiphany of the century. Do you remember what it was like to learn to write your own name?

This is today.

This is the Internet.

This is you.

And it's magic.

Brendan Kehoe
Mountain View, CA
*brendan@zen.org*

Victoria Mixon
Alameda, CA

## How to install the CD-ROM

*Macintosh*　　　　To install Cyber Patrol from the CD, drag the Cyber Patrol folder onto your hard drive, and install from your hard drive. Refer to the Read-Me file included with the software for further information.

*Windows*　　　　Copy the CP-Setup.exe file to your c: drive. Double-click on the CP-Setup.exe file from the file manager.

Cyber Patrol is frequently updated. Download the latest version of Cyber Patrol from

 http://www.cyberpatrol.com

# Acknowledgments

**T**his book would not have been finished without the help of a large number of people. Lots of folks, including Brian DeLacey, Shabbir J. Safdar, Judi Clark, Steven Hodas, Jean Armour Polly, Pat McGregor, and Glee Cady, all helped at various points during the completion of the research for the book.

In the setting of real life, I must offer thanks to: Jeff Osier, the King of Celtic music; the coffee house gang of Jen Buck, and Jimi & Christine Fosdick; my mother Alice and brother Derry, who remind me why Maine is so beautiful; my three aunts, and Aunt Sheelah in particular, for conveying to Elana and myself just why Ireland really does feel like "home;" Karen Gettman, my editor, for her patience and good spirit; Miss Elana McCoy, the soon-to-be Mrs. Kehoe, for being part of my life; and Mary Ellen Miner, a blessing to the children who are lucky enough to work with her, I thank her for her friendship

*Brendan Kehoe*

I want to extend my deepest gratitude to all of the people who so kindly invited me into their schools and classrooms: Greg Barnett, Karalee Roland, and the students of Oak Grove High School, San Jose, California; Rebecca Pevsner, Curt Chamberlain, Lynne Miles, and the students of Berkeley Montesorri Middle School, Berkeley, California; Virginia Davis, Anastasia Zita, and the students of Bryant Elementary School, San Francisco, California; and also David Katz of SJEN. To others, who allowed me to interview them at great length: Odd de Presno, Yvonne Marie Andres, Jennifer Sellers, Nancy Morgan, Blythe Bennett, Leon Crowley, and of course, Dr. Patrick O. Wheatley of the Cal Poly San Luis Obispo Computer Science Department.

In addition, I want to thank my agent, M.T. Caen, for her unending support and advice, Mary and Raché Mureau, Beth Littlefield, Jeanne Light, Paul Roach, my wonderful aunt Dolly Ann Hei, and my grandfather and lifetime birthday partner, Dan E. Weitz, for their love and great humor during these chaotic times; Kylie Murray and Doug Shaw, who arrived from Australia just in time; Jeffrey Osier, for listening to three solid weeks of non-stop monologue about how the book was progressing, for editing, converting, and formatting the text, for the loan of Jesse, and in general for his boundless patience, love, and compassion; and most especially my nieces and nephews—Ruby Mixon-Luecke, Ian and Adria Taylor, and Nik and Peter Mixon—for reminding me every moment that life is meant to be lived in a state of extraordinary wonder.

*Victoria Mixon*

"*From quiet homes and first beginning,*
*Out to the undiscovered ends,*
*There's nothing worth the wear of winning,*
*But laughter and the love of friends.*"
— Hilaire Belloc, *Verses* 'Dedicatory Ode'

# Basics

"We live in a fantasy world, a world of illusion. The great task in life is to find reality."

—Irish Murdoch

In the early 1990s, the Internet's popularity grew at a phenomenal rate. What was once a hobby for a few became a necessity for many. Universities now feel that they cannot function properly without a high-speed Net connection. Professors have to be able to share work with others, and students can stay in touch with their families, sharing the events of the day without the extra effort of finding a postal stamp and sealing an envelope.

The number of people around the world who use the Net continues to increase, limited only by the rapidly reducing cost of accessing this new medium. For less than a dollar a day, and sometimes for free through their work or school, this new global community can share thoughts and ideas at the blink of an eye.

The complexity of Cyberspace has declined to the point where the fundamental need to communicate is accessible with far less of a learning curve. Before, only computer aficionados could truly know how to use any of the Net's offerings. Yet, with the advent of the World Wide Web, and development of truly "user-friendly" software packages, the time required to *get* online has shortened, in many cases, to far less than one day—sometimes even less than an hour.

Once you're connected, however, where do you go next? There are a few fundamental concepts about the Internet that you will need to understand to take full advantage of the Net's many possibilities.

## What is the Internet?

A *network* is a set of computers and other machines all connected together so they can communicate with each other. Networks take many forms: a few personal computers can be connected to each other to share a common set of files, or a large group of computers of varying size can talk to each other across great distances. Each area of a state or country can create a network to let their local citizens correspond with other cities and towns.

Comprised of a "network of networks," the Internet links thousands of smaller networks together, so the information present on one can be reached by any other. Each network *provider*, the company that is paid for your own connection, is joined together twenty-four hours a day with other providers. For example, a provider in Portland, Maine, may maintain a connection with Boston, Massachusetts.

A collection of national *backbone* links—very fast connections in select points throughout a country—work together to reduce the time it takes for one larger area to reach another. A backbone link between Boston and New York City, or Washington D.C. and Los Angeles, provides rapid transmission over thousands of miles. In addition, the backbone links for each country are connected to those of at least one other country, thus creating a worldwide "community" of interconnected networks. A piece of information, commonly termed a *packet*, headed for Japan may pass through a backbone in San Francisco, which will allow it to cross the Pacific Ocean at remarkable speed.

All of these wires and satellites and microwave signals that make up the Internet are woven together into an invisible mesh of connectivity. A network in Hawaii doesn't necessarily know exactly how to reach one in Ireland. They do, however, know where the next destination is to reach a general area. Information bound for Europe has what's called a "default route" as its initial stepping stone. The detail of where a packet should go next starts with a general grouping of networks, and with each step the destination becomes more and more precise, until it reaches the provider for the site in question.

Routing of information is dynamic—if a network router along the way is "down," the accompanying connections adjust themselves accordingly to compensate. The goal of the Internet's design was to make it possible to react quickly to sudden changes. As network providers appear not only in more areas of the United States, but in other countries across the globe, the Net as a whole has had to adapt to this constant state of flux.

This underlying complexity of how the Internet actually works is usually invisible to those who are using it. As with the operation of a car, you don't need to know the internal workings of its engine to be able to drive one. Rather, you can learn as little or as much about it as you feel you need.

## Using the Net

To use the Internet, you will usually *log in* to a service or system with an account name and password.[1] When you're finished, you *log off* the system. While you're logged in, you often have a variety of features available to you.

*Electronic Mail*

The most frequent application of the Internet's capabilities is in the use of electronic mail, or *email*. Whether or not a hyphen is used in this word—i.e., email or *e-mail*—is open to the reader's preference. Email is simply a message being sent between one person and another. It can be a single sentence, or the equivalent of an entire book. Also, the recipient could be an individual or a group of people.

Having an email address is becoming a *de facto* standard for many people. Discussions at a cafe often include the sharing of each others' email addresses, and relatives separated by an ocean can stay in touch without worrying about the cost of travel or telephone bills.

---

1. A password is a secret word or words, sometimes coupled with numbers, known only by you, that must be given before your account can be used.

Each address adheres to a common format: a person at a certain site. The style is usually a representation of the person's name and their site, separated by an "at" sign (the '@' symbol). For example, the President of the United States can receive email at the address president@whitehouse.gov. Similarly, the address of a friend named Sven Heinicke could look something like sven@zen.org.

All addresses are not necessarily so easily guessed. Someone on America Online, a popular online service, might have the address joe123@aol.com; a student named Jennifer Hayes at an elementary school in Vermont may well have the address jhayes@mtn-view.k12.vt.us. Regardless of the actual value of an email address, they all have the same basic design.[2]

*Domains*

The second part of an email address, their site, also maintains a set structure. Each site on the Internet has its own *domain* for receiving mail, among other things. To decipher it, you need to read it from right to left. The site cygnus.com first indicates that it's the site of a company (it's part of the '.com' *top-level domain*), and then tells you the specific Internet name for that company—'cygnus' in this case. The domain for the Compuserve online service is compuserve.com; likewise, Hallmark Cards has the domain hallmark.com.

There are a number of top-level domains, the base names for all Internet domains. For example, colleges and universities are in the '.edu' domain, and U.S.

2. There are other variances, like user%site@gateway.site.com, but they're becoming much less common.

government sites are part of the '.gov' domain. However, the use of top-level domains is not limited to the United States. Sites in Ireland are in the top-level domain '.ie', and those in Canada are part of '.ca'. Lists of these top-level domains are included in most beginner's guides to the Internet.

*Mailing Lists*

Earlier, we mentioned that you can send mail to one person, or to a group of people. The latter is achieved by joining a *mailing list*. This makes it possible for mail sent to a single address to be redistributed to a number of other people.

The subjects of these mailing lists are wide and varied; issues of the day, technical questions, television programs, and other interests are all likely to have a mailing list dedicated to them. Mailing lists are also set up to distribute notices to interested parties. For example, a list can be created to let people know about the next parent-teacher conference, or upcoming musical events at a local symphony hall. Those interested in becoming part of a mailing list will send a message asking to *subscribe* to it.

Each message sent to a mailing list is passed on to everyone on that list. The *members* of the mailing list, those who have subscribed to it, can hold a conversation that is not affected by distance, physical appearance, or time—messages are read and responded to at each person's leisure.

*Usenet News*

While email is a more active form of communication—a message is delivered directly to someone—*Usenet news* delivers information passively to a large majority of Internet sites around the world. Discussions take place in separate *newsgroups*, each dedicated to a particular topic.

The names of the newsgroups are set in a hierarchy of sorts. Recreational groups all begin with 'rec.', while those related to computers start with 'comp.'. The major hierarchies for newsgroups include:

| | | |
|---|---|---|
| 🚩 | comp | Various topics related to computers. |
| 🚩 | rec | Recreational activities and hobbies. |
| 🚩 | sci | Regarding sciences of all sorts. |
| 🚩 | soc | Cultures and social issues. |
| 🚩 | talk | Debates and random discussions. |

The full name for a newsgroup starts with the main hierarchy it's a part of, and then subsequent names are added to make its name more descriptive. For example, rec.arts.movies is a popular newsgroup for commentary on the movies of the day, while rec.arts.movies.production is commonly used by people involved in actual movie creation. One of the most popular newsgroups, rec.humor.funny, is used to exchange jokes and funny stories as chosen by the group's moderator.[3]

To discuss the issues around the European Union, one might visit the group talk.politics.european-union. Likewise, to discuss the aspects of Japanese culture, soc.culture.japan is a popular choice.

3. A *moderated newsgroup* is one in which the posts are initially mailed to the person in charge of the group, who then decides if the posting should be distributed in the newsgroup.

Each of the groups in these major hierarchies were created through a voting process, which only allows them to be created through a general consensus in favor of their addition.

Another major hierarchy, the 'alt.' newsgroups, are the exception to this rule. Started by John Gilmore in the late 1980s, the alt hierarchy allows anyone to create any newsgroup they would like. This has the benefit of creating groups for topics that may not have a large enough audience to merit creation in the main hierarchy.

Thus, discussion of a particular movie recently released, a favorite author, or on a hot topic of much debate at the moment, can take place in its own alt group. The group alt.books.stephen-king is dedicated to the works of Stephen King. Immediately after the earthquake in Kobe, Japan, the group alt.current-events.kobe-quake allowed people to share experiences and keep in touch with some friends near Kobe itself.

This freedom of choice regarding newsgroup creation does have its drawbacks. Random groups, some with rather silly names, are created regularly by resourceful people who can figure out the internals of Usenet group creation. Also, discussion of controversial topics (as evidenced in the alt.sex news hierarchy) can bring otherwise objectionable information into a news site. As a result, a large number of sites refuse to carry the alt hierarchy by default, only transporting news articles for the main hierarchies.

To "read news," you can use various *newsreaders* that are available, ranging from PC- and Macintosh-specific programs to the Netscape Navigator Web browser starting with the version 2.0 release. Popular

Unix programs like rn, trn, and tin are also commonly used.

The main rule to keep in mind with respect to articles posted to newsgroups is that they are not controlled by anyone. Thus, using a software package that monitors what is being presented is often a necessity for children to be able to read news.[4]

*Transferring Files*

File Transfer Protocol, or *FTP*, was one of the earliest uses of the Internet. Files can be transmitted from one computer to another, without any of their content being changed. This makes it possible to transfer programs, images, and "compressed" files, those packed together to reduce their total size.

The customary command is, as you might expect, often named ftp. Most Internet access packages that are available include an FTP program of one sort or another. Also, a useful part of the World Wide Web, to be discussed in the next section, is its ability to FTP files using a standard Web browser.

*World Wide Web*

The most popular activity on the Net of late has been the "surfing" of the World Wide Web, more commonly termed "*the Web*." A common deterrent to using the Internet was the difficulty in finding anything on it—you had to have a fair bit of technical knowledge to even begin to use it.

With the advent of the Web, this hurdle has been avoided in large part. Sites throughout the Web have *Web pages* that contain graphically enhanced text

4. See the next chapter for a discussion of some of the various packages that are available.

(characters in italics, different font sizes, and different colors) with the addition of creative images throughout. What was a flat, black-and-white frontier gained the benefits of art and color.

To access a Web site, you will usually refer to its Universal Resource Locator, or *URL*. The format of a URL has a consistent style to it. For Web pages, they look similar to:

 http://www.zen.org/

Each is commonly started with the characters 'http://'; following that is the name of the system you want to access, and sometimes other information. For example, the URL

 http://www.zen.org/~brendan/kids.html

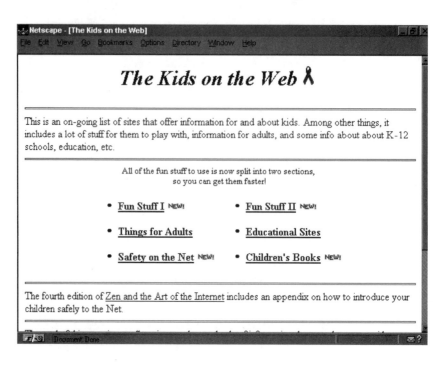

## The Kids on the Web ౯

This is an on-going list of sites that offer information for and about kids. Among other things, it includes a lot of stuff for them to play with, information for adults, and some info about about K-12 schools, education, etc.

All of the fun stuff to use is now split into two sections,
so you can get them faster!

- **Fun Stuff I** NEW!    - **Fun Stuff II** NEW!

- **Things for Adults**    - **Educational Sites**

- **Safety on the Net** NEW!    - **Children's Books** NEW!

The fourth edition of Zen and the Art of the Internet includes an appendix on how to introduce your children safely to the Net.

will bring up a Web page with a list of sites for and about kids. To reach a specific page, you need to include its full URL. If you don't remember the whole URL, you can often just visit the site's base location (as we used for the initial example above), usually called a *home page*, and move from that main home page to the subsequent page that you're looking for.

People often create their own home pages, which can hold lists of their own interests, links to other sites, a picture, or their opinion on a given issue.

The most common use of a Web page is to offer links to other sites. (These connections are often called *hyperlinks*.) This makes it possible for a page to say:

In my local paper, **The Irish Times**, I found ...

To follow the link to the Irish Times (noted by being in a bold font), you only need to click on any of the highlighted characters.

A variant to the standard "http://" URL is one that will allow you to FTP files through your Web browser. In order to use it, you must instead start your URL with "ftp://". The FTP site follows, accompanied by the path to the file in question. For example, if you wanted to visit the Washington University at St. Louis archive, without having to use a separate FTP program, the URL "ftp://wuarchive.wustl.edu/pub/" will visit the '/pub' directory on that FTP site. The page displayed will list the files in that directory, which can then be retrieved simply by clicking on the filename.

Most online services offer the ability to browse the Web as a part of their standard system. In most computer stores, you will also find a variety of commercial Web browsers for use on any type of Net connection. The number of television, radio, and newspaper advertisements that now include URLs, discussion of Web pages as standard parts of interviews, and the presence of the Web in everyday conversations has made it clear that the Internet has entered a new level of popularity.

*Live Conversations*

You can talk in "realtime" with someone else over the Internet. Beyond the possibilities of email, where your messages are separated by time, albeit sometimes quite small, actually talking with someone gives you the ability to ask and answer questions more quickly.

People have grown quite fond of the *chat areas* that are included on most online services, including America Online and Prodigy. They let people send messages back and forth that appear in a central area, so the lines sent from one person are seen by everyone. Some services also allow direct messages (termed *Instant Messages* on AOL) between two people.

A standard program for the use of the Internet is a talk utility. The command, often named talk itself, will take a person's email address and try to connect to the remote site. The end result will be a split screen, with the top half being the local person and the bottom showing what's being typed by the other.

An Internet equivalent to the chat areas on online services is the Internet Relay Chat, or *IRC*. There are few commercial services that provide access to IRC, partly because there are no controls on it. Anyone, anywhere, can talk about anything they want. While there are some areas (called chat rooms or *channels*) related to kids on occasion, children should only be allowed to use them with an adult providing supervision.

## Using Network Tools

It should be noted that you don't necessarily have to use the World Wide Web when introducing children to the Internet. Many people consider the Web the only truly usable medium for classroom teaching. However, things like email and the talk utility are equally useful.

For example, Mary Ellen Miner, the Gifted/Talented Coordinator for the Augusta School System in Augusta, Maine, used a series of online talk sessions to let her students talk to a college student in Australia. She used these conversations to teach the kids about the metric system. While telling the students about the day-to-day life in Australia (e.g., the time difference and comparing a koala to a wombat,[5] an animal not known by many of the children), the Australian student was also able to convert the students' computed metric values into pounds and inches. This made it possible for them to really understand the math problems they'd been asked to work on.

By using this tool, the class was able to learn about life outside the United States and learn a useful ability as part of their enrichment math classes. Thus, a graphical interface like the Web wasn't required—rather, plain text on a computer screen achieved the same results.

5. A marsupial native to Australia that resembles a small bear.

## Video Training

Some schools are lucky enough to employ a person who is already quite adept at the use of the Internet. However, that single person usually doesn't have the time to teach entire classrooms about the rules and processes to take full advantage of Cyberspace. Parents work to leave as many doors open as possible to their children, but also cannot be the source of all the knowledge those kids will need.

Instead, there are a few options in the area of pre-recorded video tapes that can be used. A few schools create their own, and require that students watch the tape as a class and answer some basic questions before being allowed access to the computers.

A commercial version of such a program is also available in the form of *Kids on the Internet,* from the FUTUREKIDS Computer Learning Centers and Michael Wiese Productions. A few talented kids, ages 11 and 12, get together to show how to surf the Internet, use the Net safely, and even do homework or meet new friends. There are a lot of funny bits throughout, and the kids do a wonderful job of teaching you about the Internet.[6]

The kids explain how to do a variety of tasks: sending email, browsing the Web, even a few safety tips. As can be seen at various points in the program, the kids truly enjoy their exploration and dis-

6. While educational and worthwhile on the whole, there is one minor mistake at a particular moment in the tape; a boy says that you can, among other things, "send people pictures of yourself." This should be strongly discouraged, and the tape can be paused at that point to explain the reasons why. (The next chapter addresses this and other issues of safety.)

covery of the Internet. The show closes with kids offering a few of the selling points of being online and a brief look at the steps you'll need to take to get hooked up.

To find out how to get copies of the tape, contact:

 Michael Wiese Productions
11288 Ventura Blvd., Suite 821
Studio City, CA 91604 USA
wiese@earthlink.net
http://www.earthlink.net/~mwp/
(800) 833-5738 orders in the United States and Canada
(800) 379-8808 other information
(818) 379-8799 lsewhere
(818) 986-3408 Fax

## Moving Forward

 In the coming chapters, you will learn about various ways to use the Internet with children, both at home and in the classroom. It's becoming more common for kids to be able to show adults how to find something on the Net.

This will always be the case—given the popularity and ease of use that the Internet has been gaining, kids around the world are seeing it as not only the key to their own future, but as a great resource for both schoolwork and for fun.

The reader is encouraged to choose among the many beginner's guides to the Internet that are available today (e.g., *Zen and the Art of the Internet*) to learn the complete fundamentals of the Internet. They go into far more detail and will fill in the missing gaps to give you a well-rounded understanding of the Net as a whole.

This is an ever-evolving medium. You will be given the opportunity to shape new innovative uses of it, customized to benefit your children the most. As you learn from each other, make sure that these kids do have guides and followers on their escapades in Cyberspace. They will benefit from being pointed in the right direction and be shown the best stops along the way.

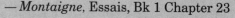

*"It should be noted that children at play are not playing about; their games should be seen as their most serious-minded activity."*

— *Montaigne*, Essais, Bk 1 Chapter 23

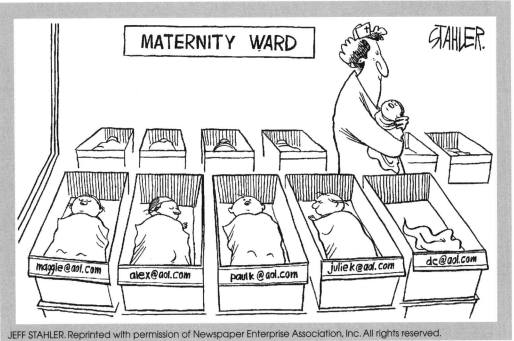

# Safety

**T**oday, the Internet presents a new and dramatic challenge for parents and teachers alike. Those who desperately want children to be protected against the more menacing aspects of life in general—and the Internet in particular—are frightened at the free reign the Net seems to hold in terms of children's vulnerability.

These guardians hear horrifying stories on the nightly news, including children meeting in person with complete strangers after talking with them on an online service. Rumors are told in passing about adult pictures being available within seconds of going online.

The computer sitting safely in the living room has, in some settings, become an open door to parents' worst nightmares. However, the Internet can indeed be a safe and fruitful place for children, as long as they are not left at the doorway to Cyberspace alone.

## General Rules

There are a few basic rules that a child has to learn before they can be out of their parents' sight. These same rules apply directly to the Internet, as well. When a child asks to go to the playground, no parent will consider allowing them to go alone. An older brother or sister, parent, or other guardian must go with them.

Similarly, the Internet is not a perfect haven without its own risks. By teaching kids to follow these simple rules, you will help prevent the more common ways children are endangered on the Net.

• **Don't give out personal information**. Your real name, address, and phone number are private; just as you wouldn't give them to strangers on the street, you shouldn't do the same on the Internet. Strangers don't need to know where kids go to school, when parents come home from work, or when kids are going on vacation.

• **Tell a teacher or parent about new friends**. A new friend found on the Net is a wonderful thing; pen pals, whether written on paper or through electronic mail, help kids get a feel for the size of the world around them. However, new friends shouldn't discourage a child to tell anyone about them, particularly their parents.

• **Don't arrange face-to-face meetings alone**. If a child believes they've found a new friend on the

Net, and would like to meet them in person, at the very least make sure you go with them. You should coordinate the meeting yourself, with the friend or that friend's parents.

- **Don't believe everything you read online**. While honesty is often the best policy, there are those out in Cyberspace who are not quite what they claim to be. A girl could really be a boy, or vice-versa. People may not always trust you, either—they don't know if you are who you say you are. Don't be paranoid, but at the same time, don't leap to conclusions.

- **Don't give out your password**. The reason passwords were created was to help keep people's information and identity to themselves. By giving someone else your password, you are in effect doing the same thing as handing out the key to your home. Some online services, and some Web pages, ask you for a "password" to access their information. Above all, don't give them the same password that you have for the system you're using.

- **If something or someone makes you feel bad, tell someone about it**. Whenever a child encounters a situation online that makes them feel uncomfortable, "strange," nervous, or threatened, make sure they know to tell someone—a parent, teacher, whomever—what has them feeling funny.

- **Find out how to block things you don't like**. Most online services allow people to selectively block areas that they feel are not appropriate for children. There are also a number of software packages available to help do this in general.

## Protective Software

There is a drawback to the wealth of knowledge available on the Internet, accessible at the click of a key (or a mouse). What some may consider information of "public interest" may well be offensive or objectionable to others. Finding the line that separates these two opinions is impossible.

While governments try to help guide the decision as to what is and is not acceptable, parents and teachers must choose for themselves what they do and do not want their children to be able to see, read, or hear. There is, of course, no replacement for a parent actively using the Internet with their child. However, using a package of this type will give you the ability to add an extra safety net around a visit into Cyberspace.

*Cyber Patrol*

One of the more popular choices available today is Cyber Patrol, from Microsystems Software. Offered for both the PC and the Macintosh, Cyber Patrol monitors the activity of anything on your computer. By including it as part of your system's boot process, the software can watch what a user is doing, to make sure that they don't happen upon the more <objectionable content>. Major online services like CompuServe and Prodigy have selected to use Cyber Patrol as one of the features of their own systems. (CompuServe offers its users a free copy of the software and a free one-year subscription to the monthly updates of the CyberNOT block list.)

Above and beyond the "standard" levels of protection, Cyber Patrol can also track the time used for a specific application and be configured to only allow use of specific programs during particular times of the day. Its bundled CyberNOT Block List gives parents and teachers an excellent starting point, by letting them decide which of a pre-selected set of sites and resources should be blocked. Items on the list can be specifically noted as being allowed, to make the package heed a particular family's beliefs and values.

People can subscribe to the CyberNOT Block List, which comes as part of Cyber Patrol with an initial trial six-month subscription. The software itself can download the weekly updates of the list. Users are strongly encouraged to notify Microsystems of newly discovered sites that are strong candidates to be included on the list—however, a stringent research process is performed before sites are arbitrarily added.

In the back of the book, you'll find a CD-ROM with a copy of Cyber Patrol for both the PC and the Macintosh, along with instructions on how to use it. It's been included to give you the opportunity to experiment with this sort of software and work it into your school's system or set it up at home.

Cyber Patrol is frequently updated. Download the latest version of Cyber Patrol from

 http://www.cyberpatrol.com

For further information about Cyber Patrol, you can contact its creators at:

 Microsystems Software, Inc.
600 Worcester Rd
Framingham, MA 01701 USA
info@microsys.om
http://www.cyberpatrol.com/
(800) 489-2001 in the US and Canada
(508) 879-9000 otherwise
(508) 626-8515 Fax

*CYBERSitter*

Created by Solid Oak Software, CYBERSitter is another package providing monitoring capabilities for your child's Internet travels. Parents are able to decide how the system should react to a visit to a potentially objectionable site. Rather than just arbitrarily block access, the system can be adjusted to do a combination of blocking the site and alerting the user to that fact.

Thus, a site may just be "inaccessible," as far as the person using the computer is concerned. A password is used to guard against modification of the use of CYBERSitter, or adjustment of its settings. Available for PCs, the software can be set up with ease and also offers the additional step of censoring particular words or phrases. When they're matched, the noted words or phrases are subsequently "X'd" out, allowing the reader to use the rest of the page or document. A document would include "XXXX" instead of a swear word that's frowned upon.

A log of all of the user's travels while using the Internet can also be maintained, for later review. Thus, you can sit down and talk with your child if you see that they tried to look at something that isn't necessarily "right" for them. Certain Usenet newsgroups and online chat areas are also tagged as being inappropriate for kids. This will keep children out of the more "adult" chat areas and newsgroups related to topics that may not be appropriate for their reading.

Children can also be prevented from giving out personal information online like their full name, their home address, or phone number.

A free trial version of CYBERSitter is available online by visiting the Solid Oak Software Web page.

You can also receive further information by contacting them at:

Solid Oak InterGO and KinderGuard
Software, Inc.
PO Box 6826
Santa Barbara, CA 93160  USA
sales@solidoak.com
http://www.solidoak.com/cyrsitter.htm
(800) 388-2761 in the US and Canada
(805) 967-9853 outside the US
(805) 967-1614 Fax

Designed "for the classroom," but also quite useful at home, InterGO from TeacherSoft is a well-designed graphical interface to Cyberspace. Initially available for Windows 95, with Windows 3.1 and Macintosh versions soon to follow, the software acts as an entry point to doing research with the Internet.

A wealth of information is pre-categorized for you, in subjects varying from history to music, government to mathematics. Newly discovered sites can be noted in a custom bookcase in the InterGO Library, to help schools of particular cultures collect information particularly useful to their setting and surroundings.

InterGO was fashioned to allow more than one user to draw on its benefits, by having separate user IDs and passwords. Each "account" maintains its own settings. Parents and teachers can qualify a particular Web page as only being suitable for someone above a certain age and note the user's age in their account profile.

Integrated in the InterGO package is Kinder-Guard, a feature that facilitates protection of kids while they go exploring. Certain pictures, words, and other content are analyzed, set to block those deemed inappropriate for the current user's age group. Coupled with the ability to specifically allow content that would otherwise be blocked, InterGO carries with it a selective, cooperative approach to child protection.

To learn more about InterGO, contact:

TeacherSoft, Inc.
903 East 18th Street, Suite 230
Plano, TX 75074 USA
TeacherSoft@teachersoft.com
http://www.teachersoft.com/
(214) 424-7882
(214) 424-5503 (Fax)

*The Internet Filter*

The Internet Filter, for systems running Windows 3.1, will monitor all Internet traffic from your computer. Certain messages, Usenet newsgroups, Web pages, or information from specific hosts can be logged and blocked, if desired.

The tool, available in two versions, is easy to install and operates quietly in the background on your computer. "Version Zero" of Internet Filter is available for free on the Internet. It does have a limited range of activity—the configuration has been pre-set and is not as extensive as "Version One," a package available for a low price from Turnet Investigations, Research and Communications.

With Version One, you have the additional ability to have the system send mail to a parent or teacher whenever a particular site, newsgroup, or phrase has been accessed or discovered. The objectionable words or phrases are "X'd" out, as with CYBERSitter. However, the package can also be set up to not deny or block such access—instead, it will simply make a lot entry and possibly notify you when detected.

You can find copies of Version Zero on a variety of FTP sites, including ftp.coast.net in the directory '/SimTel/win3/internet' and ftp.cdrom.com in '/pub/ simtel/win3/internet', both as the file 'netfilt.zip'. The pkunzip DOS tool is used to unpack the software, which is then quickly installed by running the program 'FILTINST.CFG'.

To find out more about the Internet Filter, or buy a copy of Internet Filter Version One, you can contact the distributors at:

Turner Investigation, Research and Communications
Box 151-3456 Dunbar St.
Vancouver, BC V65 2C2 Canada
bturner@direct.ca
http://www.xmission.com/~seer/jdksoftware/netfilt.html
(604) 733-5095

*iscreen!*

In Redwood City, California, the NetView Communications company does regular rating and indexing of Internet sites on a diverse set of criteria. Parents and teachers alike can, with the NetView *iscreen!* software, decide what should and should not be allowed based on a number of issues, including content related to sex, violence, nudity, obscenity, and a variety of others.

Specific user IDs and passwords are used to create a custom profile for each user. With Windows-based copies available initially, soon followed by a Macintosh version, *iscreen*! lets you override the rating of a particular page if you so desire. Communities and cultures with different opinions can each use this sort of software, adjusting it to the thoughts and beliefs that are most applicable.

For a copy of *iscreen!*, you can visit the NetView home page or contact them at:

NetView Communications
558 Brewster Ave
Redwood City, CA 94063 USA
ccc@netview.com
http://www.netview.com/
(415) 299-9016
(415) 299-0522 Fax

*Net Nanny*

While many packages address only children's safety on the Internet, Net Nanny from the Trove Investment Corporation goes a step further. Any program running on your PC, using the Net or not, is monitored for particular words, phrases, content, and sites based on a custom list created by the parent. This allows you to decide what you do and don't want your children to receive or see, while at the same time avoiding the hot issue of who can choose the qualifiers for "objectionable" material.

Any time a particular key word is detected by Net Nanny, it will automatically exit the application being used and make note of the discovery in a log file for later review. The list of items to be caught can include personal information or even credit cards—this will help avoid problems where kids try to order things online by offering a credit card number for payment.

Given its perspective on your PC, Net Nanny will monitor children's activities while using online services like America Online, Prodigy, and others. To find out more, contact the creators of Net Nanny at:

> Net Nanny Ltd.
> Main Floor - 525 Seymour St
> Vancouver, BC V6B 3H7 Canada
> netnanny@netnanny.com
> http://www.netnanny.com/
> (800) 340-7177 order line for US and Canada
> (604) 662-8522
> (604) 662-8525 Fax

*Rated-PG*

Similar to Net Nanny in some respects, the Rated-PG package from PC DataPower is a complete system manager that gives users the ability to not only control Web page access, but also general use of the computer. Parents and teachers can block access to CD-ROMs and applications that are considered sexually explicit or too violent, preventing installation or possibly limiting operation to certain users.

Each child can be allocated a fixed time period of use for the computer, or even for a specific game or tool. Their daily, weekly, or monthly usage can be preset, and reports generated showing all of their activity, by a variety of criteria. This can help make sure that children are using the computer for the right purpose when they're left unsupervised. In addition, the cost of online services will be reduced by keeping the total time available for them within certain bounds.

The sheer size of the Internet can be daunting for users who want to try to protect their children from unexpected or unhealthy content. As a starting point, with Rated-PG, parents and teachers can decide what

Internet sites are allowable, and which should be specifically restricted. By only permitting the use of sites that are known to be safe, the users can feel more secure in the system's use.

A larger collection of sites on the Internet can also be blocked by adding an optional list that's included as part of the package. Users are free to add other sites, or remove those that they feel should be accessible. If desired, a subscription is available to receive periodic updates to the list. Customers can register with PC DataPower and get two initial updates for free.

The classification of the sites is not important— whether it's to a Web site, an FTP archive, or a gopher server, any connections over the Internet on that computer are controlled in the background, without seriously hindering the speed of the system.

Passwords can be used to prevent access to particular files and entire groups of programs from being used, as needed. Stringent security makes it more difficult for the control of the system to be defeated, thus addressing the common problem of children outmaneuvering what was set up for their own protection.

Rated-PG is available for PCs running either Windows 3.1 or Windows 95. Its interface is very user-friendly; a simple mouse-oriented set of windows allows the user to install it quickly and find the information they need. To find out more about Rated-PG, contact:

PC DataPower
1891 Alton Parkway
Irvine, CA 92606-4902 USA
info@ratedpg.com
http://www.ratedpg.com/
(714) 553-8883
(714) 852-8136

*Net Shepherd*     There are a number of approaches to creating a safety system for the Internet. Some note specific sites around the Net as those that should be "avoided;" still others use a ratings system, similar to movie ratings.

Net Shepherd uses a password-based browsing system, similar to that used by InterGO, that allows a parent or teacher to decide if a site is appropriate for the person accessing it. Whether on a PC running the various Windows operating systems, or on a Macintosh, users of Net Shepherd have their access denied to a page or site rated inappropriate for them.

Each account can maintain its own database of site ratings or fall back on an assigned Ratings Service database. By default, the system will block access to a page that has not been given a rating—the administrator of the system can make this wholesale blockage be disabled, if they wish.

Net Shepherd can be downloaded over the Net, by visiting the Web page

 http://www.shepherd.net/

You can contact the maintainers of the package at:

Net Shepherd Inc.
202, 1212 31st Ave, NE
Calgary, Alberta T2E 7S8 Canada
info@shepherd.net
http://www.shepherd.net/
(403) 250-5310
(403) 250-9689

*SurfWatch*

One of the earliest packages that offered the blocking of offensive Internet sites was SurfWatch. Initially available only for the Macintosh, but now also available for Windows PCs, the software uses an in-depth list of sites that are considered inappropriate for children, and are thus blocked from access.

For example, if a child tries to visit the Web page for an adult men's magazine, a box appears on the window telling the user that the site has been blocked by SurfWatch. People can subscribe to monthly updates of the list of offensive sites, and schools can receive educational discounts for site-wide updates.

Also part of the CompuServe Internet In a Box for Kids package, SurfWatch can be integrated to general Internet access and block not only Web pages, but also the many Usenet newsgroups that are often not valid areas for children's eyes.

To learn more about SurfWatch, you can contact the software developers at:

SurfWatch Software
175 South San Antonio Road, Suite 102
Los Altos, CA 94022 USA
info@surfwatch.com
http://www.surfwatch.com/
(800) 458-6600 in the US and Canada
(415) 948-9500
(415) 948-9577 Fax

## Online Services

The publicity surrounding the safety of children on the Internet has not been ignored by popular online services. Since they are quite often a family's initial entry into Cyberspace, systems like America Online, CompuServe, and Prodigy must all enhance their services to provide parents and teachers with an initial form of protection for their kids.

Along with the various protective software packages, most online services now take the extra step to protect children while they're running through the vast expanse of Cyberspace.

*America Online*

One of the more popular features of America Online is their online chat rooms. In these areas, people can get together in groups and talk about particular topics, ask each other questions, or just have random conversations with those who happen by.

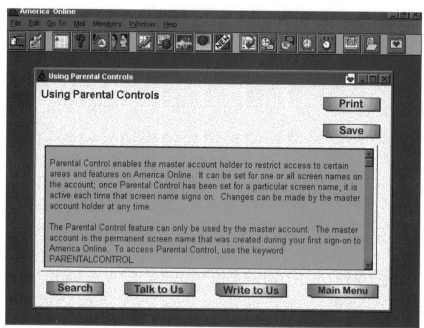

Parents feel intimidated allowing their children to use these chat areas, however, due to potential dangers in talking with strangers. If you feel that setting up some ground rules with your child isn't enough, America Online (*AOL*) has another step you can take.

Each AOL account is composed of a "master" account screen name and a few other accompanying screen names. Only the master account can alter the settings for the whole group, including parental control of the chat areas.

After logging into AOL, choose the "Parental Control" option of the "Members" initial menu. You will be given a list of each of the screen names for your account, and in corresponding boxes the choices of which chat options are available to that name. A box containing the letter 'X' indicates that a particular chat option has been disabled for that screen name. A final click on OK will save the settings and make them take effect. The "Parental Control" box is also available in all of the online chat areas, among the list of other rooms and finding out who's in each one.

Thus, younger children can still use AOL but not receive Instant Messages—one or more sentences sent directly to that person's screen in a pop-up window—from strangers, or visit worrisome chat areas.

An area on America Online has been set aside for kids; by visiting the Kids Only section, children can share their hobbies, go exploring, and share stories with other kids. The area is heavily monitored to make sure that its name accurately reflects its contents. When children want to visit the Kids Chat area, they are greeted by a message telling children that they should not receive an email message from a stranger that might have something attached to it. (The most common case is an obscene photograph.) The kids are told to have their parents forward that message on to "TOS Kids,"[1] who will then review it and return it for reading only if it's not indecent.

Parents can go to the keyword "parent review" for more information about protecting their children on AOL.

*CompuServe*        CompuServe has put quite a bit of time and effort into making sure that children are safe on their service. Their Parental Controls area is password-controlled (using a password other than the one for the account itself). If a parent forgets the password, the

1. *TOS* stands for Terms of Service, the review team who enforce the various rules of use for America Online.

initial setup also includes the entering of a particular question and its answer, to verify that the person talking to CompuServe support is in fact the parent or teacher who initially set the options.

The adult setting up the account can choose to block certain areas on CompuServe itself (type GO AOCL to review the default list) and those accessed on the Internet. A copy of the Cyber Patrol package is available for free from CompuServe, including a free one-year subscription to the CyberNOT Block List.

Kids can now access CompuServe by way of their new WOW! service. Initially available for Windows 95, and the Macintosh soon after, WOW! gives families the ability to use the Internet by way of a cartoon interface. Access is separated into the use of adults and children, with control functionality that allows for restriction of certain types of information.

A strong multimedia design to WOW! complements it with sounds and graphics, which add zest to being online. Web sites on the Internet are currently limited by the speed of the recipient's Net connection. Since the files that provide this environment are actually stored locally on a CD-ROM, the time required to actually see and hear them is drastically reduced.

When adults use WOW!, they are given access to a number of the Net's many facets, including viewing Web sites and sending email. Children are given an entertaining setting, with fun characters guiding the way. Similar to America Online, an extension to the original CompuServe account setup adds the capability to have six separate users all based on the same flat subscription rate. Thus, a full family can pay a single monthly fee for its use.

CompuServe, as a whole, provides parental control with more than this custom tool. In addition, the Parental Controls Center[2] takes advantage of the Cyber Patrol software package. Access to certain sections of CompuServe can be blocked, and, using Cyber Patrol, Web sites and Web content is also monitored. Usenet newsgroups, telnet, and FTP are also included in the variety of services that can be controlled through the Parental Controls Center. Together, WOW! and the Center help offer an online service that lets parents assist and guide their children.

Also offered by CompuServe, and available in many computer software stores, is the *Internet In a Box for Kids*. Intended for children ages 8 to 14, *Internet In a Box for Kids* puts together a Web browser, email, low-cost Internet access, safety software, and an instructional video. Attached to the package is the SurfWatch blocking package, to deny access to objectionable material. The end result is a well-collected set of tools that help bring children safely into the online world. For people who do not have systems capable of running the WOW! package, *Internet In a Box for Kids* may well be the next best solution.

*Prodigy*

Two areas, the Kids Zone and Teen Turf, are set up to allow children to talk with each other. Topics of all sorts—homework, pets, even baseball cards—can be discussed to no end.

The main account for Prodigy can easily block the use of their Web browser, if you'd rather not have it

2. On CompuServe, type GO CONTROLS.

available. Simply choose the Access Control option of their main World Wide Web area.

## Safety Projects

With more and more children using the Internet every day, its seemingly random content is becoming more and more controversial. There are a variety of projects that have been started recently that aim to address the problem; among them are the CyberAngels effort and attempts to do voluntary rating of Web sites.

*CyberAngels*

In mid-1995, volunteers gathered together to found the CyberAngels Project. Based on the Alliance of Guardian Angels, a non-profit organization of volunteers that started in the late 1970s, the CyberAngels aim to provide a similar grass-roots safety net in Cyberspace. The original Guardian Angels worked to protect people by making citizen's arrests—crimes being committed were no longer ignored when they were seen firsthand. A group of only a few people working together to protect those in the community around them grew extensively, now numbering in the thousands in countries across North America.

The similarities between people travelling on subway systems and those exploring Cyberspace became pronounced as more people began to be online. The "apparent lawlessness" of the Internet prompted them to investigate what steps they could take to help take care of this new virtual community.

The infrastructure of this new effort is the volunteers themselves. Each person commits to spend at least two hours each week surfing through the Net, looking for areas that have what they believe to be unacceptable content or activity—objectionable pictures, chat areas, and the like. Occasionally the CyberAngels will notify volunteers of a certain area that should be investigated.

Child abuse and pedophilia, child pornography, software piracy, and various forms of online fraud are among the kinds of material that their members pursue. Just as it's impossible to guard an entire city, Cyberspace is a wide and continually growing society. However, each effort contributes to the whole; the work of a few people can benefit many that they may never actually meet.

To volunteer with the CyberAngels, or to find out more about them, write to the address

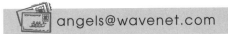 angels@wavenet.com

*SafeSurf and PICS*

The Platform for Internet Content Selection (PICS), led by the World Wide Web Consortium, is a project aimed at allowing the rating of Web sites. They are working to develop the technical methods needed to achieve this goal. The end result will make it possible not only for sites to label their own contents with a given rating, but also to allow third parties to create ratings collections of their own.

A parents' online organization, SafeSurf, is developing the actual application of the SafeSurf Internet Rating System. One of the fundamental goals in the design of this technology is to make sure it is relatively easy to use. Parents and teachers will need to use this functionality, without having an in-depth technical grasp of exactly how it is deployed and executed.

Most of the various software packages that are available follow this voluntary rating. Termed the *SafeSurf Wave*, a particular line is added as part of the Web document's content. People can get a Wave for their own page by visiting the SafeSurf home page at the URL

http://www.safesurf.com/

After providing information about the page's content and recommended age range of visitors, the system answers with the line that should be added to the HTML document; by simply copying the line from the Web browser into the actual file being rated, the Web page's maintainer can make their site known to be child-safe, or to contain information that is likely to offend or be judged inappropriate for children.

Sites that have been approved by SafeSurf are frequently highlighted as part of the SafeSurf page; their "Kids Wave" page lists Web pages that benefit younger children and a collection of sites that will be of use for older kids and for parents. The "S.E.R.F Page" offers teachers a wealth of information for educators.

To find out more about SafeSurf and the PICS standard, you can visit the SafeSurf home page at the previously mentioned URL. You can subscribe to a monthly newsletter (which is also available online at their Web site) that provides reviews of kids' sites, safety tips, and keep, you up-to-date regarding their rating system.

If you'd like to learn more about SafeSurf and the evolution of the PICS ratings standard, they can be reached at:

SafeSurf
16032 Sherman Way Suite 58
Van Nuys, CA 91406 USA
http://www.safesurf.com/
SafeSurf@aol.com
(818) 902-9390

*"Parents who know their children's teachers and help with the homework and teach their kids right from wrong—these parents make all the difference."*

— *President Bill Clinton*

# Getting Connected

"Technology . . . the knack of so arranging the world that we need not experience it."

—*Max Frisch*, Home Faber

**W**ith all of the publicity the Internet receives on a daily basis, people react with the desire to join in on the excitement. Children hear about their friends using the Net, families want to make it available for their kids to use it for their homework, and schools are driven to be online. The next logical step, however, is often the most difficult: how to actually "get connected."

There are a number of possibilities to reach this end goal. Online services of various forms, network providers, and links sponsored by local colleges and corporations all help bring people closer to taking full advantage of the Internet.

To balance the cost of one option over another, you will need to guess what you really want to spend for the service. The flat monthly rate for a full-fledged network provider is the preference for schools and companies, while the hourly rate for an online service is the common choice of periodic home use. If your work or classes depend upon the ability to reference things on the Net, you will need to work out a full connection or solid network account at a local provider. However, the lower expense of a pre-created online service usually fills the general needs of most first-time users.

Once you've come to the decision of which method of access to use, you will be able to begin measuring one feature against the other and, perhaps, switch to an alternative after a period of time. You just need to get started and try one approach, so you can see what your online needs really are.

## The Essentials

To take advantage of the Internet, you usually need at least a computer and a modem. If you're accessing it at work or school, your PC or Macintosh commonly has a wired link to a main "entry point" for your site. That way, you're able to use the Net right away, without waiting for the phone to dial or your computer to connect.

The prices of modems have been falling dramatically; what used to be over $100 for a moderately fast speed connection has been reduced to between twenty and forty dollars. In the late 1980s, a 9600 baud[1]

1. Bits per second is the term often used to describe the speed of a modem; "baud" is the more common description.

modem was considered certainly fast enough for most people. Today, a modem must be at least "14.4" ("fourteen-four," a modem at 14,400 baud) or "28.8" (at 28,800 baud) to be considered usable in many settings. Given the size of the information being transferred— no longer just words, but images and sounds as well— this extra speed is required to receive everything in a reasonable amount of time.

The *bandwidth*, how much it can carry, of most Net connections has grown exponentially. It's now possible to send large pictures, transfer files that are the equivalent of a few reams of paper, and transmit live sound in a fraction of the time it did only two years ago.

With the modem or Net connection, some software is required on your computer. Many systems now include a collection of tools pre-installed for your use. Network providers often offer packages as part of your sign-up costs; for example, Netcom and Pipeline, two of the larger network providers in the United States, have created custom interfaces that give you access to the many points of interest in the use of the Internet.

## Online Services

One of the newer industries that has blossomed within the last decade is the offering of an online service, which carries with it the ability to use the many facets of the Internet. Most of these services now include a variety of features including email, Web access, and online chat. Making the proper choice is usually based on the needs of a particular user, the price of a particular service, and their own preferences regarding the service's layout and presentation.

Three of the larger online services in the United States are America Online, CompuServe, and Prodigy. Some of those same services also provide access in other countries as well. Each of the three has a similar price range, yet the price is still not low enough—after an initial amount of time, an hourly cost of two to three dollars per hour can cause bills to grow at an alarming rate. All things must be used with moderation.

An interesting twist from the American standards is the offering of America Online in the United Kingdom. (No, that's not meant to be confusing.) Secondary schools in the UK can apply for free accounts, with unlimited access. This allows teachers to make full use of AOL's Education area, in particular, without fear of high costs.

The disks and CD-ROMs that have the software for these services are often attached to magazines, included in mass mailings, and available at local bookstores. They include everything you will need to get connected, arrange for payment, and start using the service. Many computers include the software for many of the services as a standard part of what's packaged with your computer when you buy it.

The offerings of each online service are similar, with a few exceptions on occasion. For example, the Web browser used on one may not have the same features as that of another. Advertisements and newspaper articles also regularly include their choice of the "better" online service.

You can reach each of the services directly at:

| | | |
|---|---|---|
|  | America Online | 800/827-6364 703/448-8700 |
| | America Online in the UK: 0800 279 1234 | |
| | CompuServe | 800/848-8990 614/529-1340 |
| | Prodigy | 800/776-8449 914/448-8000 |

The advent of other online services, with a new one appearing each year or two, helps contribute to the variety and popularity of the Net. Lowering costs and increased dialup locations are both bringing the Internet into more homes.

## Online Accounts

The next step up from basic online services is the use of an account on a local site. Most universities and colleges are willing to give an account to a local teacher whose school has not yet been able to be hooked up. Likewise, some companies make accounts available to people on an as-needed basis; many firms allow their employees to request accounts for their husbands or wives. A number of sites that are connected to the Net offer access to people on an as-needed basis, or for a set fee equal to or lower than online services. Finally, in some areas, there are "FreeNet" sites, which are created to make it possible for members of a community to get online. The use of these systems is free of a monthly cost, although there are some limits in what you're able to do.

Often, these accounts require some knowledge of the Unix operating system, while others have a menu-based system to help make it easier to use. To find out where you can possibly receive a low-cost account locally, ask nearby universities and colleges, and talk to friends who work for companies that are probably hooked up to the Internet. (There may be a local FreeNet that your friends will have heard of and may even use themselves.)

## Network Providers

A network provider is frequently thought of as someone who provides your site with a full-time connection to the Internet. While in the larger scale of things this is true—companies and schools connecting their whole site require this level of service—others seek to make the full scope of the Internet available to people, beyond what traditional online services may offer.

Two such providers, Netcom and Pipeline, have experienced unprecedented growth in recent years. What was originally a team of one or two dozen people working together to create a possible solution to Internet availability, has increased to thousands of employees with connectivity points in hundreds of cities. The level of service they provide has expanded accordingly. Custom software packages, technical support lines, and continued addition of new access points—commonly termed Points of Presence, or *POPs*—made an interesting idea for a project become a fully functional business model.

People who find that the customary online services are "not enough" turn to these mid-level providers for their access. The prices are usually relatively low—perhaps $20 to $30 each month for unlimited access—and prove to be worth the cost with the increased range of use.

You can contact the two providers we mentioned above at:

To find out about providers that offer service in

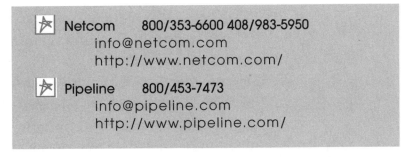

your local area, consult local newspapers, the yellow pages, and the variety of Internet magazines that should be available in local bookstores.

You can also visit the Yahoo[2] Web page and do a search with the words internet provider. This will yield a long list of sites that provide service not only in the United States, but also various countries around the world.

## Full-Time Connections

If you need a connection that is usable by a group of computers simultaneously, setting up a full-time link is the better choice. This makes it possible for people to work as a team or independently on projects, using email, file transfer, and the Web on separate machines. Each is isolated from the other, so one person can visit a particular Web page while another drafts an email message to a colleague.

While the cost of a full-time connection can be prohibitive for individuals, most offices and schools are able to find funding for this level of service. With the possibilities that are opened up for many people by way of a single, larger capacity link, the end benefit proves worthwhile.

The equipment to actually maintain this full-time connection is frequently expensive and difficult to use. Some companies are willing to sponsor the actual wiring of schools in their area. Also, some providers will do the maintenance of the equipment for a set fee. Finally, you can dedicate a computer and phone line to a full-time connection over a standard 14.4 or 28.8

2. Point your Web browser at the URL http://www.yahoo.com/.

modem. This will let you to maintain your own Web server, have email delivered locally, and a variety of other tasks. This approach requires a fair bit of technical proficiency, however, and usually proves frustrating over time for all but the most experienced computer users.

Many schools take the position of having the children do the maintenance of the site themselves. With a few teachers that are well-versed enough to teach new students, this can give children the opportunity to gain experience and feel like they're involved in the site's actual "Net presence."

Contact your local provider for information about how they offer full-time connections, including their standard prices and the details of what kind of links they offer.

*"The new electronic interdependence recreates the world in the image of a global village."*
— *Marshall McLuhan*, Understanding Media

# Resources on the Net

**4**

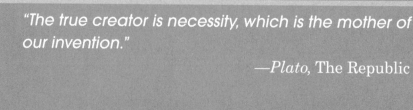

"The true creator is necessity, which is the mother of our invention."

—*Plato*, The Republic

**T**he number of resources available online to K-12 educators and parents is staggering. They range from simple Web sites with fun stuff for kids, to international organizations doing cutting-edge research in K-12 educational technology. The organizations listed here are some of the biggies, but this is by no means all. Hopefully, you can use these organizations as starting points, and once you're familiar with them you'll be comfortable searching the Web for more sites and groups.

## KIDLINK

KIDLINK is by far the most comprehensive international online organization that involves K-12-aged children directly. KIDLINK maintains KIDCAFE, an online forum for children between 10 and 15 years old, in six languages around the world. KIDLINK also offers two mailing lists for educators and parents: KIDLEADER and KIDPROJ. KIDLEADER runs adult coordinator conferences, in which the discussions center around how to use the KIDLINK resource in the classroom. KIDPROJ runs on-going brainstorming sessions to develop projects appropriate for K-12-aged children. KIDLINK and its various mailing lists serve approximately 50,000 children worldwide.

With a global coordination team of 80 volunteers, KIDLINK operates as an entirely volunteer-run, non-profit grassroots organization.

KIDLINK provides a wonderful, supportive community for K-12 educators and parents, and KID-CAFE is the number one forum for kids online. KIDLINK started out on SciNet, a conference network in Toronto, Canada, in May of 1990 and moved to the Internet within a few months. Since then, the English language KIDCAFE has expanded into twenty-eight public conferences conducted in six languages and a private IRC chat network.

KIDLINK recognizes the variety of societies involved around the world and respects all views on social, ethical, legal, and moral issues.

Children are free to express their opinions however they like on KIDCAFE, but KIDLINK does expect goodwill to be extended toward all participants. KIDLINK does not promote specific solutions to any current issues or any political perspectives.

What KIDLINK does do is monitor KIDCAFE to make sure that adults don't try to contact children

inappropriately through it. Also, although there have
been requests to start a KIDCAFE for younger children, at this point KIDCAFE is restricted to children
between the ages of 10 and 15 years old.

Every May, KIDLINK holds their annual, international birthday party so that students, parents, and
educators from all over the world can celebrate their
connection to each other and their global accomplish-
ments for the year.

Co-founder Odd de Presno says that his vision of
KIDLINK is about the wonderful energy he felt planning KIDLINK with children online, an energy he
thinks it would have been a shame to leave untapped.

Visit the KIDLINK Web page at

 http://www.kidlink.org/

To subscribe to **KIDLINK**, send email to:

listserv@vm1.nodak.edu

with a blank subject line and the message:

> subscribe kidlink *Your Name*
>
> get kidlink generals

in the body of the letter.

To get a list of back issues of the **KIDLINK** newsletter, include this line also:

> get kidlink master

To unsubscribe, send email to the same address with the line

> signoff kidlink

in the body of the letter.

## The Global Schoolhouse (GSH)

GSH is a four-year-old program that links schools from around the world by videoconference. GSH was conceived of in 1992 as a worldwide K-12 community linked by videoconference to "transform the way we work, live, and learn."

The non-profit Global SchoolNet Foundation, which has existed for twelve years, is the umbrella organization for the Global Schoolhouse and its services. GSH was originally called Free Educational Electronic Mail (*FrEdMail*), but in 1992 they received an NFS grant to create the Global Schoolhouse in order to demonstrate using live video over the Internet, bringing distant classes together. In April of 1993, the original GSH—Jefferson Junior High of Oceanside, California, Cedar Bluff Middle School of Knoxville, Tennessee, Long Branch Elementary School of Arlington, Virginia, and Oldfield House School of Hampton, in the United Kingdom—was demonstrated over the Internet during the U.S. National Science & Technology Week. This was also the first CU-SeeMe videoconference.

GSH runs a variety of mailing lists, including GlobalWatch and SchoolNet. GlobalWatch serves as a bulletin board for new projects and events, with a free membership of several thousand. SchoolNet is a subscription service of moderated news groups that are free of sexism, racism, violence, and other material inappropriate to K-12-aged children, with a paid membership of approximately 300. You or your school can subscribe to SchoolNet for $250 a year, or else your school district or state can subscribe for a negotiated amount. For instance, if you live in North Carolina, your state is already subscribed to School-Net. SchoolNet is also bundled on some Internet servers such as BBN in Massachusetts and The Link.

Yvonne Marie Andres, GSH President and Curriculum Director, is a tremendously helpful resource to any educator, particularly if you're interested in videoconferencing. She says the GSH focuses on giving teachers the strategies they need to integrate the Internet into their teaching—not just to add to the curriculum, but to replace some parts of it. She calls it "Internet-style Learning," and believes there are components of it that are more powerful than the tools of traditional teaching.

Andres gives the example of a letter she recently received in which the teacher of a class of blind students thanked her for making current information available to her students. The teacher told Andres that, in the past, by the time information was translated into Braille or other media that her students could use, it was already old. Through the Internet, blind students now have equal access to current information as well as communication with students around the world.

Although GSH's NSF grant expired in 1994, in November of 1995 Bill Gates announced a partnership between GSH and Microsoft, which means that GSH can count on funding for the future.

In conjunction with Cisco Systems Inc. and MCI Corporation, GSH is also sponsoring an International CyberFair for schools worldwide as a part of the Internet 1996 World Exposition.

To subscribe to GlobalWatch, send email to

 lists@gsn.org

with a blank subject line and the message:

subscribe global-watch Your Name

in the body of the letter. To unsubscribe from the list, write to the same address with a blank subject line and the message

unsubscribe global-watch

in the body of the letter. To subscribe to SchoolNet, contact Al Rogers at the email address

 webmaster@schoolnet.org

For more information, the Global SchoolNet Foundation can be contacted at:

Global Schoolhouse/Global SchoolNet Foundation
7040 Avenida Encinas 104-281
Carlsbad, CA 92009  USA
Attn: Yvonne Andres
helper@gsn.org
http://www.gsn.org/
(619) 433-3413
(619) 721-2930 Fax

## CU-SeeMe

 CU-SeeMe free software was developed at Cornell University by Dick Cogger, who envisioned CU-SeeMe as a live, interactive videoconferencing tool for K-12 education. It was introduced in April of 1993 when the first demonstration of the (K-12) Global Schoolhouse was presented over the Internet during U.S. National Science & Technology Week.

CU-SeeMe developed alongside the Global Schoolhouse, and right now one of their joint ventures is a pilot project in which schoolchildren in Australia are interviewed live on ABC's World News Now, broadcast in the evening in the United States.

 CU-SeeMe members are encouraged to use the mailing list in a variety of ways. You may post events for other K-12 schools to participate in, publish lesson plans using live interactive video in the K-12 classroom, explore the uses other educators have found for interactive video and ways to fit them into your own curriculum, ask for critique on your video presentation, or discuss innovative uses of CU-SeeMe in long-distance learning. In particular, CU-SeeMe moderators would like to receive messages that describe how you use the Internet in your classroom and how others might be able to do the same.

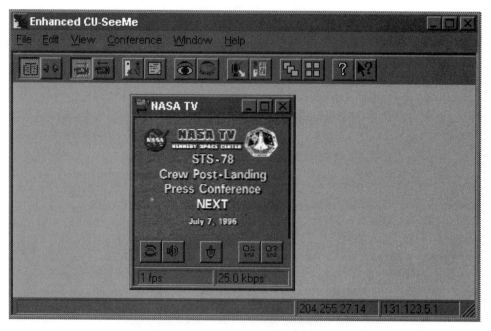

To subscribe to the CU-SeeMe schools mailing list, send email to lists@gsn.org with a blank subject line and the message

> subscribe cuseeme-schools *Your Name*

in the body of the letter. The same address is used for unsubscribing from the list; the message should contain the line

> unsubscribe cuseeme-schools *Your Name*

White Pine Software sells an Enhanced CU-SeeMe package. To find out more, point your Web browser at the URL

 http://www.cu-seeme.com/

Also, you can write them at the address info@wpine.com, or euro_info@wpine.com for European sales.

You can also download free CU-SeeMe software for the PC and Macintosh from the FTP site

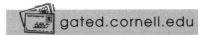 gated.cornell.edu

in the directory '/pub/CU-SeeMe'.

## Consortium for School Networking (CoSN)

CoSN is an educators' forum that promotes NII, the new National Information Infrastructure, in schools. CoSN is dedicated to bringing educators up-to-date information on how to get quick, easy, and cost-effective access to the Internet and on-line resources. CoSN also serves as a discussion list and sounding board for teachers, school administrators, librarians, and other professionals involved in school networking, addressing the issues of federal telecommunications laws and policies, as well as state legislation regarding NII Goals 2000.

CoSN has a membership of approximately 750. You can post anything on the subject of school networking, which includes announcements of events, requests for help, and topics for discussion. On a random day, you might find a message from an experienced school administrator asking for technical advice on setting up a network, or a series of messages between teachers discussing whether or not to restrict students' access to some areas of the Internet.

Every year, CoSN holds an annual conference in a major city in the United States, at which professionals from the field of technology in the K-12 classroom share their knowledge with educators from all over the country. The CoSN conference is one of the more highly-esteemed educational technology conferences in educational technology.

CoSN also automatically posts a FAQ to all members on the 1st and 15th of each month. You can get a copy of it by sending email to

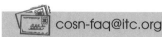

cosn-faq@itc.org

or by using gopher to look on list.cren.net under "mailing list archives: CoSN Discussion List," or by looking on the CoSN gopher under "CoSN Gopher Welcomes You!".

To become a member of CoSN, send email to the address listproc@listproc.net with a blank subject line and the message:

subscribe COSNDISC

in the body of the letter. To unsubscribe, write to the same address with the single line

unsubscribe COSNDISC

in the body of the letter.

To post a message to all members of CoSN, send it to:

cosndisc@list.cren.net

For information on the FAQ, send email to Jay Pfaffman at pfaffman@itc.org. For additional information on CoSN in general, they can be contacted at:

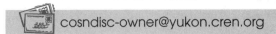
Consortium for School Networking
1555 Connecticut NW, Suite 200
Washington, DC 20036 USA
membership@cosn.org
http://www.cosn.org/
(202) 466-6296

If you have trouble getting a response from CoSN for any reason, send email to

cosndisc-owner@yukon.cren.org

## Information Infrastructure and Technology Administration

IITA is a four-year-old cross-federal-agency program to interactively bring information and educational materials to K-12 educators and parents. IITA is an exceptionally useful science resource.

IITA has four on-going goals: to provide as much information over as broad a range of subjects as possible for teachers who are going online; to run online interactive science programs through NASA; to disseminate print materials; and to find low-cost networking solutions for schools.

Information is provided primarily through the IITA Web site and at educational conferences.

The online interactive programs run for up to three months, and each program is focused around a particular NASA project such as the Hubble Space Telescope project. The goal is to bring science and real-life content directly to the classroom. Text and data files from each project, as well as a Teacher's Guide and related classroom materials, are available online.

In addition, educators and parents can sign up for several mailing lists. From one, educators and parents receive regular journal reports from scientists working on the current project. On another, educators and parents can discuss how they're using the current program in their curriculum. On the third, educators and parents can send email to the scientists, which is filtered through software and human volunteers who reply directly to questions whenever possible and, for questions IITA can't answer, forward the question to the scientists—one question out of each batch (this protects the scientists from being overwhelmed).

Three videos are available for free from the NASA Teacher Resource Center. The first video, "Global Quest: The Internet in the Classroom," promotes bringing the Internet to the K-12 classroom. The second video, "Connecting to the Future," explains how to build a networking infrastructure in your community to bring the Internet into the classroom. The third video, released on May 1, 1996, "Global Quest II: Teaching With the Internet," shows how to integrate the Internet into classroom curriculum.

IITA has developed models for low-cost networking solutions and made them available online through the Quest program at Langley. You can contact IITA Director Jennifer Sellers for more information.

IITA also maintains the K12 Internet Initiative, and within that Initiative is a document called FYI-22, specifically for K-12 end users of the Internet.[1]

Founding co-president Dennis Bybee feels that the new educational activities in the classroom are breaking down the barriers of time, distance, and location. He says that although the traditional educational paradigm is industry-based, the current educational paradigm is information-based, and in an information-based paradigm, technology makes teachers more productive.

IITA began with the passage of then-Senator Al Gore's High-Performance Computing bill. The Educational Outreach component of that bill specifically addresses bringing the Internet into the classroom. IITA is a department of the ISN, the Internet School Networking group of the Internet Engineering Task Force, or *IETF*. For more about the ISN, you can visit the IETF Web page at

 http://www.ietf.org/

and look on the page regarding their "working groups."

IITA is associated through ISN with ISOC, the Internet Society, operated out of Reston, Virginia. (ISOC isn't solely aimed at K-12 educators, but it is the umbrella organization for the Internet as a whole). You can visit the IITA Web site at the URL

 http://quest.arc.nasa.gov/

1. A copy of the FYI is available at the URL ftp://ds.internic.net/rfc/rfc1578.txt.

To learn more about the NASA Ames K-12 project in general, drop by their Web server at a similar URL:

 http://quest.arc.nasa.gov/net-learning.html

For information on the videos, send a blank message to the address

 video-info@quest.arc.nasa.gov

For more information, contact Jennifer Sellers at:

Jennifer Sellers
NASA Ames Research Center
Mail Stop 233-18
Moffett Field, CA 94035-1000 USA
sellers@quest.arc.nasa.gov
(520) 615-9788

# AskERIC
# Educational Resources Information Center

AskERIC is an online Question-&-Answer service based on the Educational Resources Information Center (ERIC) database at Syracuse University, Syracuse, New York. Educators and parents can send in questions on any topic and receive answers personally researched by the AskERIC staff.

AskERIC, like KIDLINK, is well-known and respected throughout the online educational community. AskERIC handles between 300 and 700 questions a week, up from a range of between 50 and 300 from when they started in 1993. The Q&A Department has a staff of four full-time employees, who receive regular assistance from between fifteen and twenty people at ERIC. In addition to the Q&A, AskERIC maintains a Virtual Library and a Research & Development Department.

AskERIC is a Sun Site Repository with $100,000 of donated Sun Microsystems equipment, but because it's considered "exploratory," it still only gets funding from year-to-year grants. Unfortunately, this means that the original goal of providing full texts online is economically unfeasible, so instead they write abstracts of articles and ERIC documents, such as conference papers that professionals submit to the database.

AskERIC began six years ago at the ERIC Clearinghouse on Information & Technology, where task forces were looking for ways to make full text available online. ERIC is actually a database of sixteen subject-specific clearinghouses, such as Disabilities, Early Childhood Education, and Math & Science.

Mary Beth McKee of the Syracuse University Information Studies Department met with Bob Stonehill, then Director of ERIC Systems, and they made plans to create a Virtual Library as their contribution to the emerging online community. With a grant of $50,000 from the Department of Education and the help of Syracuse University students, they hired a full-time employee and opened the original AskERIC help line in November, 1992.

AskERIC Coordinator Nancy Morgan sees AskERIC reaching "front-line" teachers, the ones in the K-12 classroom with a need for fast, concrete research.

Send your questions to AskERIC either by filling out the form on their Web page at

 http://ericir.syr.edu/

or via email at the address

 askeric@ericir.syr.edu

You can contact the AskERIC Coordinator Nancy Morgan at:

 ERIC, Clearinghouse on Information & Technology
AskERIC
4-194 Center for Science & Technology
Syracuse University
Syracuse, NY 13244-1400 USA
nmorgan@ericir.syr.edu
(315) 443-3640
(315) 443-5448 Fax

## ICONNECT

ICONNECT is the umbrella organization for four different programs for K-12 educators, both teachers and librarians, and parents: IBASICS, Curriculum Connections, Mini-grants for Librarians, and KidsConnect. ICONNECT is sponsored by AASL, the American Association of School Librarians, as a part of ALA, the American Library Association.

IBASICS is an online course for K-12 educators and parents that helps you get familiar with the Internet. Currently, a first-level Basics course is offered, through which lessons are emailed to participants with both information and exercises, and both Intermediate and Advanced courses are planned for the near future.

Curriculum Connections is a good way for K-12 educators and parents to get a feel for the Web. Librarians around the country have chosen their favorite Web sites for a variety of subjects, such as dinosaurs and space, which are then categorized under headings like Social Studies and Science. These sites are meant to serve as examples of each librarian's policy on what's appropriate for K-12-aged children and can be used as a model for your own choices. Each site is chosen specifically because it has not only good information, but has no links to sites that may be inappropriate.

Mini-grants are awarded to members of the AASL for projects in K-12 education. The ICONNECT Web site has information on application procedures and previous grant winners.

KidsConnect, modeled on AskERIC, is a Q&A service for kids. KidsConnect is run entirely by volunteer librarians around the United States, under the management of one full-time employee in the ERIC building, and is funded by Microsoft. KidsConnect has trained librarians all over the country to research and answer children's questions on library subjects, ranging from print resources to "Where can I find information on...?"

KidsConnect went public in April of 1996 during National Library Week, after three pilot programs throughout the previous months, so it's still stabilizing. Regular updates regarding KidsConnect can be received by sending mail to the address

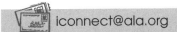 iconnect@ala.org

Questions for KidsConnect should go to the address

 AskKC@iconnect.syr.edu

You can also visit the ICONNECT Web page (particularly for information on mini-grants for librarians) at the URL

 http://ericir.syr.edu/ICONN/ihome.html

For more information, contact Blythe Bennett at:

 ERIC, Clearinghouse on Information & Technology
ICONNECT
4-194 Center for Science & Technology
Syracuse University
Syracuse, NY 13244-1400 USA
Attn: Blythe Bennett
blythe@ericir.syr.edu
(800) 464-9107 inside the United States

## International Society for Technology in Education

ISTE was conceived of as the official technology-accrediting group for all levels of education. ISTE's corporate vision is called TEST, Technology-Enriched Schools of Tomorrow, and, like CoSN and IITA, advocates using technology to improve K-12 education. Primarily, ISTE is a good place to get printed information for reference material for your school, as well as information on annual Tel-Ed conferences.

ISTE is a non-profit organization with a membership of over 60,000, and is based at the University of Oregon in Eugene. The ISTE's publications branch does $3 million of business every year, providing educators and parents with how-to information on different aspects of educational technology.

ISTE offers three types of services: projects, professional enrichment services, and an outreach program.

Project services cover issues like school reform, research, and accreditation recommendations for Colleges of Education. They also make contributions to national and international initiatives on educational technology.

ISTE provides professional enrichment services like special interest groups and Distance Education Courses. For example, Teacher Education, a special interest group of about 1,000 members, conducts teacher training at conferences around the country. And SIG-Tel, ISTE's Special Interest Group for Telecommunications, has a mailing list membership of about 3,000. The outreach program involves both a Private Sector Council and a particular program called The Critical-Connection, which specializes in fostering partnerships between schools and businesses. For parents in business who would like to help their children's school, this is a particularly important resource.

ISTE began in 1989 in the U.S. as a consolidation of two previous international computer associations that dated back twenty years: ICCE, the International Council for Computing & Education, a K-12 organization, and IACE, the International Association of Computing & Education, a higher-education organization focused on teacher training.

Every year ISTE, along with FACE (Florida Association for Computers in Education), organizes Tel-Ed, the annual International Conference on Telecommunications in Education. The 1995 conference was held at Ft. Lauderdale, Florida, while the 1996 conference is scheduled for December in Tampa, Florida. Tel-Ed

is highly attended by K-12 educators and by administrators of organizations like IITA and Web66.

To subscribe to SIG-Tel, send mail to their mail
server at SIGTEL-L@unmvma.unm.edu with a blank subject line and the message:

> subscribe sigtel-l *Your Name*

in the body of the letter. To unsubscribe, instead send
the message

> unsubscribe sigtel-l

in the body of a letter to the same address.

To order published materials or to join the ISTE,
you can reach them at:

 International Society for Technology in Education
Agate Hall
1787 Agate Street
University of Oregon
Eugene, OR 97403-1923 USA
iste@oregon.uoregon.edu
http://isteonline.uoregon.edu/
(800) 336-5191

## National Center for Supercomputing Applications (NCSA)

In 1992, the NCSA Education Group published the
first edition of the online manual, *An Incomplete
Guide to the Internet and Other Telecommunications
Opportunities, Especially for Teachers and Students K-
12*, intended to help teachers understand what the
Internet is and how to use it.

There are two parts to *An Incomplete Guide*: a reference section for different Internet tools, and a categorized guide for Internet-related resources, particularly curriculum. Although both parts have been updated bi-annually over the last six years, the guide to resources will be discontinued as of this year.

*An Incomplete Guide* is a thorough and exhaustive (around 300 printed pages) explanation of all aspects of the Internet, from a basic discussion of "What is the Internet?" to specific instructions on using Unix and such tools as FTP and the Eudora email package, as well as tutorials on the tools Archie, Gopher, and Veronica. It's valuable reference material for the K-12 educator interested in learning the technical aspects of educational technology.

NCSA is associated with the University of Illinois and is funded in part by the NSF.

A copy of *An Incomplete Guide* is available in Postscript and Microsoft Word formats via FTP from

 ftp.ncsa.uiuc.edu

in the directory

Education/Education_Resources

For more information, contact Pam Joop at:

NCSA Education Outreach
Computing Applications Building, Room 263
605 East Springfield Avenue
Champagne, IL 61821 USA
Attn: Pam Joop
i-guide@ncsa.uiuc.edu
(217) 224-0409

## Classroom Connect

Classroom Connect is a hardcopy (not online) newsletter aimed at the K-12 online educator and published nine times a year. Classroom Connect costs $39/year and contains regular departments on lesson plans, available grants, and listings of educational resources. In addition, Classroom Connect runs features on everything from Acceptable Use Policies to free software to FTP.

Because it's printed, Classroom Connect can be an easy way for educators and parents to collect information about using technology in K-12 education, if you're not yet comfortable sorting through that kind of information online.

Classroom Connect lesson plan ideas center around four defined areas: proposed grade level, objectives, necessary materials, and the actual procedure, along with extensions to the procedure.

A new selection of available grants is listed in each issue, along with information on the goals and the mailing addresses of the foundations.

Every issue also contains a full page of listings of educational Web sites and mailing lists, including brief descriptions of each resource and email addresses. This page is designed to be cut out and saved.

Editorial Consultant Gregory Giagnocavo says that Classroom Connect likes to consider themselves the premiere K-12 newsletter that focuses on using computers to enhance education.

To submit articles or editorials to Classroom Connect, send email to Chris Noonan Sturm at the address

cnsturm@classroom.net

To request a free trial subscription of Classroom Connect, write connect@classroom.net. Finally, to receive the Frequently Asked Questions, send email to

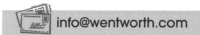

info@wentworth.com

with a blank subject line and the command

send crc-faq

in the body of the message.

For more information, contact Classroom Connect at:

Classroom Connect
c/o Wentworth Worldwide Media
1866 Colonial Village Lane
PO Box 10488
Lancaster, PA 17605-0488 USA
connect@classroom.net
http://www.classroom.net/
(800) 638-1639 in the United States
(717) 393-1000 elsewhere
(717) 393-5752 Fax

## Global Village Schools (GVS) Institute

Every year, GVS Institute holds an annual conference in a major city in the U.S.A., bringing together K-12 educators from around the country to brainstorm on the future of technology in the K-12 classroom. This is conceptual planning stuff, as opposed to practical exercise. The conference includes seminars on relevant emerging technologies, roundtable discussions led by professionals in school networking, and workshops focused on designing the new educational environment.

Announcements for the GVS Institute Annual Conference are posted on CoSN, although the amount of the registration fee is not generally included in the announcement. The 1996 conference was held in March in San Francisco, California.

Dr. Leon Crowley of the University of Oklahoma describes the GVS Institute Conference as a gathering for creators of the next generations of learning and teaching, a conference about reform, redesign, restructuring, re-engineering, invention, imagination, and education in the Information Age.

The first Global Village Schools (GVS) Conference was held in 1993 as a cooperative project between the Meckleburger Group, the University of Oklahoma, and the Center for Educational Leadership and Technology (CELT). This conference was the origin of the GVS Institute.

For more information, contact Dr. Leon Crowley at:

 University of Oklahoma
555 Constitution Avenue
Norman, OK 73037 USA
Attn: Dr. Leon Crowley
gvs@uoknor.edu
(405) 325-1711
(405) 325-1824 Fax

# Web66

Web66 is primarily known for the Web66 International WWW Schools Directory, which contains the Internet's oldest and most extraordinary list of school Web sites around the world, over 2,750 sites from fifty countries by early 1996 (this is double the number from November of 1995 and nearly four times the number from early 1995). Web66 is also a mailing list for discussing the use of the World Wide Web in the K-12 classroom, although it does focus on schools that produce Web information. Discussion includes questions, ideas, solutions, and projects that have to do with technical, administrative, and curricular information.

Among other things, Web66 contains: a hotlist of new Web sites for K-12 education; clickable maps of Australia, Canada, Europe, Japan, and the United States; the Classroom Internet Server Cookbook with step-by-step recipes for setting up a Web site and email server; and the Network Construction Set, which describes Ethernet network components along with instructions for setting up school LANs and WANs with Internet capabilities.

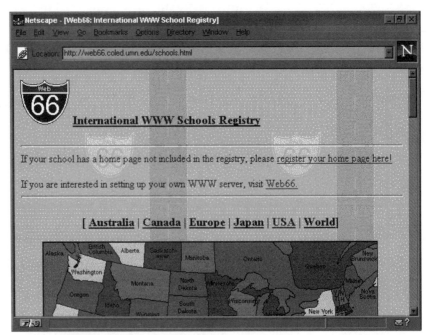

You can visit Web66 at

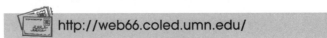

http://web66.coled.umn.edu/

with your Web browser. To register your school's Web site with Web66, send email to

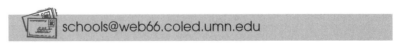

schools@web66.coled.umn.edu

For more information, contact Stephen E. Collins at:

Web66
152 Shepherd Lab
100 Union Street SE
Minneapolis, MN 55455  USA
Attn: Stephen E. Collins
sec@web66.coled.umn.edu
http://web66.coled.umn.edu/Webmaster.html
(612) 625-6817 Fax

# Children Accessing Controversial Information (CACI)

CACI was created in July of 1995 as a discussion group among adults regarding the safety of children on the Internet.

Today, CACI has a membership of over 500 people. Discussion topics include the Cyberporn controversy, appropriate community efforts to set standards for children's protection, and how to deal with pedophiles on the Internet. On a random day, you might find a message from a teacher discussing what boundaries are reasonable for their students or one from a parent asking how dangerous the Internet really is to their child.

To subscribe to CACI, send email to

 caci-request@cygnus.com

with a blank subject line and the message

    subscribe

in the body of the letter. To unsubscribe from the list, use the line

    unsubscribe

in your message. The mailing list is also available in "digest" form, where the mail sent to CACI are periodically grouped together into a single message. To join the digest version of the list, subscribe as before, but send your message to the address

 caci-digest-request@cygnus.com

instead.

To post a message to the mailing list, send it to:

caci@cygnus.com

For more information, contact the current maintainer of the CACI list at

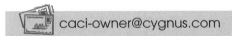

caci-owner@cygnus.com

## GENII
## Group Exploring the National Information Infrastructure

GENII was established in 1994 at Deakin University in Victoria, Australia, as a clearinghouse for training K-12 classroom teachers in technical skills. GENII's goal is to make it easier for educators to integrate the Internet into lesson plans by giving them technical expertise and practical support.

In particular, the GENII Web page could become the most important doorway into K-12 educational resources on the Internet. Although it's still under construction, this Web page provides links to a wide range of Web sites that K-12 educators and parents can use in their curriculum or research and promises to become the most trafficked entry point to the Web by the K-12 adult educational community.

GENII is a voluntary network of over seventy educators helping K-12 teachers develop technical skills. For instance, right now GENII offers educators online instruction in HTML, under their HTML Pilot project, which you can reach through the GENII Web page.

GENII has three major goals: to create a Virtual Faculty, to write a Curriculum, and to maintain their Web page with links to as many educational resources as possible.

The Virtual Faculty is a pool of knowledgeable educators dedicated to helping K-12 teachers acquire technical skills at your own speed. The Faculty also serves as an on-going resource to all K-12 teachers moving into online education. Their emphasis is on answering the questions that no one wants to ask for fear of seeming ignorant, on explaining technical procedures in layman's terms, and on just being supportive of teachers as you get accustomed to the Internet.

The Curriculum will be published in a series of manuals that cover such information as how to get on the Internet, what resources to look for, and how to develop lesson plans. An important piece of this Curriculum will be the section on how to write Acceptable Use Policies, which have not yet been written for many schools.

GENII also produces "The New South Polar Times," a bi-weekly newsletter written by the staff at Amundsen-Scott South Pole Station, South Pole, Antarctica.

Visit the GENII Web page at:[2]

 http://139.132.40.31/GENII/GENIIHP.html

or search the Web for 'GENII'. To add a link to GENII, send submissions to Lynn White at

 whitel@ten-nash.ten.k12.us

 2. The server for the GENII Web site will move to rice.edn.deakin.edu.au in January, 1997.

For more information, contact George Duckett at:

Deakin University
221 Burwood Highway
Burwood, Victoria 3125 Australia
gduckett@deakin.edu.au

## Cisco Educational Archive and Resources Catalog Homepage

CEARCH was created by the University of North Carolina at Chapel Hill, along with Cisco Systems, Inc. CEARCH contains the Virtual Schoolhouse, a meta-library of K-12 links, an excellent online research tool for K-12 educators and parents.

The Virtual Schoolhouse is divided into nine areas, most of them named after locations in a school. "Classrooms" has educational links sorted by subject, while "The Library" has links to libraries and other sites where books can be found, and "The Art Room" has links to museums and art exhibits. At "The Playground" you can find games and entertainment. "The Techie's Corner" has links to Web tools and authoring information, archives of software, and information on networking. Through "The Teacher's Lounge," you can find teaching resources on the Internet, and through "The Principal's Office" you can find planning and implementation resources for educational planners and administrators. Finally, through the newly-developing "Schoolhouse NOC," you can find information specifically for schools who want to get hooked up to the Internet, and "Schools and Universities on the

Internet" is a listing of elementary, secondary, and international schools.

In conjunction with the Global Schoolhouse and MCI Corporation, Cisco is also sponsoring an International CyberFair for schools worldwide as a part of the Internet 1996 World Exposition.

You can visit the Virtual Schoolhouse at the URL

 http://sunsite.unc.edu/cisco/index.html

To add a link to the Virtual Schoolhouse, send email to the address cearch@sunsite.unc.edu. For more information, you can contact the project at:

 **Cisco Education Program**
P.O. Box 14987
Research Triangle Park, NC 27709 USA
edu@cisco.com
(800) EDNTWKS Cisco Education Hotline

*"Discovery consists of seeing what everybody has seen and thinking what nobody has thought."*
— *Albert von Szent-Györgyi*
The Scientist Speculates

# The Shift in the K-12 Educational Paradigm

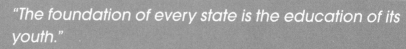

*"The foundation of every state is the education of its youth."*

—*Diogenes Laërtius*, Lives of Eminent Philosophers

**T**he biggest obstacle to computers in the K-12 classroom today centers around the educational paradigm.

It's being acted out in schools across the country, in educators who are either passively or actively reluctant to bring computers into the classroom. It's dramatized by educators trying to bring computers into the classroom, who struggle not only with practical and economic obstacles, but also with the reluctance of their colleagues. And it's epitomized in the stereotypes of the young, computer-wielding para-professional with a mouse in one hand and a revolutionary treatise in the other, squared off against the graying, angry schoolmarm and master with a blackboard pointer and a dictionary. In schools across the country, the differences in the educational paradigm, which are exaggerated by the advance of technology into the classroom, is turning into a pivotal issue.

Traditionally, the educational paradigm presents the teacher as the center of the classroom and education as rising from that source. In the new paradigm, each student is the center of his or her own learning experience and his or her education rises from a myriad number of sources throughout the classroom.

This causes problems for many teachers of the traditional school, who worry about losing control of the classroom. Along with a focal point for learning, the traditional teacher also serves as the focal point for all activities, giving the teacher control over the energy level and behavior of the children.

In the new paradigm, the teacher is no longer the focal point for activity. As anyone who's ever been in a grammar school room can tell you, it's easy for children's energy level to get out of control. And when the energy is out of control, behavior normally follows. At what point is the teacher then transformed from educator to cop? And is it more efficient for the teacher to retain control of educational material, and therefore of the children, than to disseminate control of the materials and then battle to retain control of the children?

There are two issues at stake here: who controls the students' learning experience, and how much technology is appropriate for K-12 education. And when you've decided how you feel about the issues, there is still the question of how to integrate the Internet into your curriculum.

## Training Teachers in the New Educational Model

There are two types of problems that school administrators have to deal with in bringing technology into the classroom: 1) resources and 2) teaching educators to understand the concept of computers in the classroom.

Many teachers have trouble with the paradigm shift from one model to another—from a teacher-centered model to a student-centered one. When you look into training your teachers, you have to show them that the point is not just to put technology in schools, but to advance the educational model based on the opportunity of technology.

The schools need to show the teachers that technology is a means—not an end—to creating a community.

First, let's look at training teachers who are already willing to work toward bringing technology into their classrooms. You need to cover several areas, including minimal technical skills, curriculum integration, and the paradigm shift.

In addressing the paradigm shift, you'll need to give your teachers an idea of how the new educational model benefits both the students and the learning environment. As Rebecca Pevsner of the Berkeley Montesorri Middle School pointed out, the new model pivots on teaching the students personal responsibility. This lesson is an important part of introducing computers to any classroom.

This is something you'll have to teach your educators to do. It won't happen overnight—particularly

when you're dealing with kids who have been in the school system for a long time without facing this issue—but teaching students to accept responsibility for their behavior is worth the concentrated focus that it takes. When the teacher is no longer responsible for monitoring the children's behavior, the entire class is freed up to explore new opportunities for education.

It's important for teachers to hold the students accountable for all of their classroom behavior in the first few weeks, whether they're using the computers or not. Students need to learn that it's not just what they do online, but their attitude toward behavior in general that's getting an overhaul.

They might try to override you on this, but don't let it rattle you. If you have to, call a halt to everything long enough to discuss a problem that's gotten out of hand, like an argument between two students or repeated failure to do homework. Bring the whole class into a dialogue about it.

**Doonesbury**                                          BY GARRY TRUDEAU

Have confidence in yourself—you don't have to get the kids to arrive at a solution, just to conduct a reasonable discussion about different sides of the issue. You are still the authority. You still make the rules and enforce them. The difference is that, in getting the class involved each time a rule is broken, in a rational and non-judgmental way, you teach them to look at their own and others' behavior in terms of responsibility rather than simply consequences. You also teach them to think things through before they act and to trust their own perceptions of what's right and wrong.

Don't let the discussion get out of hand. By marking a clear beginning and end to it yourself, you let them know that this is not a game, but something you take quite seriously.

And don't be discouraged if your students resist. They're bound by a children's secret code of honor to test your boundaries, particularly when you appear to have narrowed the field on them. Stick with it.

You'll find that your class will pick up the concept in ways you haven't even anticipated, so long as you maintain a firm guideline on your expectations for their behavior and an open mind when you call for discussion. In this way, you can recreate the climate in your classroom that allows for an educational model in which the students have greater freedom. Once they figure this out, you can relax your attention to the new model. They're on track.

The best way to handle teachers who are reluctant or unwilling to accept technology in the classroom is with respect. You may or may not be able to change their minds. This may or may not be essential to your school as a whole. The important thing to focus on is that you all have jobs to do in the field of education, and it's not such a bad thing if teachers come at their jobs from different angles.

The other thing to keep in mind is that they may be voicing very real concerns that haven't occurred to you yet. Lend them an ear. Maybe what they're saying is something you've heard a thousand times before. But it's always possible that there's something in their perspective that will shed a new light on your school's entire experience with educational technology. Your patience and willingness to listen can, if nothing else, make relations between proponents of the new model and guardians of the old model congenial.

The fact is, within a very few number of years, your students are going to know far more about educational technology than any of us in the field today. Try to keep from putting too much stock in your own

*"Yes, we do have the authority to regulate you."*

Drawing by Bruce Eric Kaplan; © 1996 The New Yorker Magazine, Inc

perspective right now, as it's guaranteed to change, and by all means keep your sense of humor.

As far as designing a training program for your teachers or for educators in your district, the San Jose Educational Network training program serves as an excellent model and an example of known success.

SJEN has trained around 50 percent of the teachers in the city of San Jose through a summer training program. This was on the teachers' volunteer time, but each high school teacher who went through the training got a computer for their class. They've also trained around 150 more teachers from the middle and elementary schools in San Jose, with the understanding that the schools will provide the computers.

This year, SJEN plans to train 1,000 teachers in a summer program. This is double the number of teachers from last year and the year before, but SJEN expects things to go easier this year, because last year they were struggling just to get everyone online and this year the schools already are.

Teachers get involved through their districts. SJEN notifies the districts of the allocation for each one, and they recruit the teachers they feel are most suited for the training program.

There's a five-day technical training course with a set curriculum, focusing on telecommunications. The SJEN courses are taught for three weeks until they've trained all of the teachers, in addition to elective courses in specific applications like Microsoft Word. Then, they'll bring them all together for three days of final training in the second phase, which is more conceptual. They break the teachers up into eighty groups of twelve, with one technical volunteer for each group, and take them through a process to create projects to implement computers in the curriculum. They do team-building, talk about what's possible and what's not regarding constraints in the classroom, and practice problem solving. The point is to build a community of educators and an online support system.

These thousand teachers are approximately 15 percent of all the teachers in Santa Clara County. SJEN also gives them training in how to pass on what they've learned, and a big part of the training is that all of the teachers are committed to curriculum projects that will be documented on their classes'

home pages, to promote networking among the teachers and provide assistance for newer teachers.

## The Role of the Internet in K-12 Education

The educational community falls into two camps on either side of the issue of technology in the K-12 classroom.

On one side are administrators, educational technology leaders, new teachers with a background in computers, and educators and parents with a personal vision of the future of computers in the K-12 classroom.

These include principals who work against the odds to get funding and donations to bring computer networks into their schools; principals like Karalee Roland of Oak Grove High School, who makes up her mind what she wants and then simply finds a way to finance it.

They also include leaders in the field of educational technology who work with schools to realize President Clinton's goal of NetDay 96; professionals with backgrounds in everything from management to teaching to computer technology.

They include the new wave of teachers—and all succeeding waves—who, unlike older teachers, have grown up with computers in their lives and now graduate from college with practical experience on computers and an idea of what computers can bring to the educational model.

Finally, they include teachers of all ages and backgrounds, from all parts of the world, who have a personal ideological stake in bringing computers into the classroom and who dedicate their time, above and beyond the call of duty, to blazing a trail into the technological future of K-12 education; people like Virginia Davis of Bryant Elementary School, who worries that the middle and high schools her kids are heading for don't have computers and says that 'eventually' isn't soon enough for her.

On the other side of the issue are administrators, educators, and parents with a background in traditional or alternative teaching methods, who question whether the advent of the computer is necessarily the advent of progress.

These include principals with budgets to balance, discipline problems to resolve, alternatives to consider, and a fine line to walk between federal cutbacks and a continuous flow of new studies on K-12 education.

These also include some Waldorf and home-schooling educators and parents, for whom the emphasis on computers in the classroom may glorify technology at the expense of the holistic growth of children. Such educators often keep a suspicious eye on technological advances—particularly in the K-12 classroom—in order to monitor the effect of such technology on the environment and on the fate of their own values in the social picture. Although these educators are not necessarily Neo-Luddites, they share many values in common with the Luddites, in particular an overriding concern with society as a whole and with situations in which technology is promoted without taking into account social welfare.

Additionally, these include many teachers who have been in the public education system for twenty years or more, teachers who have seen new programs appear every year, have been trained and re-trained in the same methods under a variety of names, who have become leery of new ideas and, sometimes, bitter about having to defend themselves against what seems to add up to a waste of their teaching time. They know that what matters is not what you call it, but how it affects the children.

The common ground between all of these groups is clear: the welfare of the students. Whether it's emphasized through interest in the environment or technology, through traditional educational means or cutting-edge research in how children learn, it boils down to the same thing. Everyone wants what's best for the children.

In order to identify the ways in which several groups with one goal wind up with conflicting agendas, it's important to identify the ideals behind the agendas.

Certain ideals fuel the drive toward technology in the classroom. Among them are the ideals of stretching the limits of education, of putting the power of learning into the hands of the students, of keeping the internal cultures of schools abreast of the external cultures of the society, and of recognizing that most of us can no longer consider ourselves citizens of many different countries, but only of a single global village. Perhaps the most powerful of these ideals is the hope that, by equipping children today with certain tools for conflict resolution—such as regular, daily international contact with children around the world, which can only be realistically acquired through the Internet—the adults of tomorrow will be able to find new ways for our world to seek peace.

Of course, ideals also fuel resistance to technology in the K-12 classroom. Foremost among these is the awareness that technology does not always equal improvement. Stretching the limits of education can be accomplished in a variety of ways: by taking advantage of the natural development of the human brain, by challenging children to learn physically as well as intellectually, by exploring the role of archetypal understanding in the learning process, and by moving the classroom out of an enclosed environment—of which the computer terminal is a stereotype—into daily life.

It's true that these models may also allow for putting the power of learning into the hands of the students and for decentralizing authority so that children learn conflict resolution as an integral part of their education. And these models may allow for an educational paradigm in which the welfare of the planet is stressed as a part of the children's awareness of their immediate environment.

What non-technical models do not allow for, which technical models do, is regular individual contact between two children on either side of the planet. Although the children of one culture may be thoroughly educated in the ways of another culture, there is an element of daily life that can only be experienced firsthand.

The Internet cannot send children across the globe, but it can do the next best thing: it can put them in contact with 'foreign' children who can describe 'foreign' life firsthand to them, in children's own words and through their own perceptions. It can allow two children on either side of the planet to strike up a friendship on a daily basis, sharing experiences like the trip to school in the morning, what they did over the weekend, what their best friend said yesterday. These children have the opportunity of forming a life-long bond based on common personalities and values, a bond that supersedes the limits of culture and location.

As a child, you may have had a pen pal in another country, someone with whom you shared many of the epiphanies and downfalls of growing up. As an adult, you may have had a chance to meet your pen pal, to put a face and voice, mannerisms and quirks, to the friend you'd made through the mail. How many of you, however, found that the bond of exchanging letters once or twice a month for a few years out of childhood was not strong enough to last into adulthood? How many regret the limits that kept that friendship on the page?

When international mail first reached a level of efficiency that allowed for the original pen pal organizations, it was a revolutionary step. For the first time in children's lives, time and distance were no longer the deciding factor in who could become friends with whom. For educators and parents all over the world, a new perspective on peace seemed possible.

Historically, modern society has had one official perspective on the kind of revolutionary peace that global contact among friends makes possible. That perspective was exemplified in a landmark episode in World War I, in which French and German soldiers came out of their trenches on Christmas Eve, 1914, to share the holiday. They shared food, customs, humor, and inevitably friendship. When they were given orders to fire on one another the following day, they refused. This was in direct violation of the international law against Fraternizing With the Enemy During Wartime. The problem? The human inclination to reconcile rather than to destroy.

This human inclination is the hope of those who want to bring a new kind of peace to the world through the Internet. It's not the automation of data or technology for technology's sake, that makes the difference in the quality of education. It's human contact. The medium is impersonal: simply metal and plastic, a box with a video screen hiding a rack of silicon chips and a wire into a wall. However, what it allows is contact between more humans worldwide than any medium yet invented. This is important to remember: it's not contact between computers, but between people. And the more people are involved at a manageable level in any given project, the more inherent humanity there is to that project.

For example, when a KIDLINK teacher read a note intended for one of her students and felt 'somehow wrong' about it, she posted it on the KIDLINK educators' mailing list and asked for advice from educators and parents around the world. The note was, ostensibly, from another child, but the adults involved almost unanimously agreed that there was 'something wrong' with it. Although the teacher herself couldn't put her finger on it, the Internet allowed her to ask advice from such a wide variety of educators and parents that she found several who could, in fact, put their finger on what was wrong and explain it clearly.

In this case, it was technology that freed one teacher from having to rely on either her own solitary judgement, or on some pre-defined standard, and brought the element of human judgement into the picture. Through the efforts of adults all over the world, one child was protected from inappropriate adult contact and many educators learned something new about the way children think and how to identify the difference between that and the way adults think. Without the Internet, this would not have been possible.

Along the same lines, technology frees children from pre-defined standards of judgement and brings the element of humanity to their perceptions of lives they've never experienced. Although pen pals are normally encouraged by schools, the percentage of time a class can devote to writing short letters is considerably less than the percentage of time a class can spend sharing their education and communicating about vital current affairs with their companions across the world.

During the war on Bosnia-Herzegovina, children in America learned firsthand what war was like for children in former Yugoslavia. During firestorms in Australia, Australian children described their experiences to other children around the world. In countless international projects aimed at raising awareness to ecology, such as KIDLINK's Blue Print Earth, children put their heads together to brainstorm on practical ideas that can be implemented by everyone to protect their shared planet.

Like children everywhere, the children involved in these projects make friends with each other. In fact, many projects list communication and alliances as primary goals. Because once children have made friends with children of distant countries—once they've spent a large chunk of their childhood educations thinking, writing, and talking about each other's daily lives, making human contact with each other beyond the boundaries of geography—they'll grow up to have a vested interest in protecting the welfare of people on far sides of the globe. If their friends are endangered, will waging war seem like a reasonable solution to political conflict? Or will their experiences in understanding other cultures have given these children conflict resolution skills applicable to all areas of life and society? Will heads of state who are inclined to wage war be required by necessity to seek peace?

The hope that such a simple solution will force complex military systems into alternatives to war sounds naive—after all, there are always ways to manipulate patriotism into nationalism and nationalism into territorialism.

However, naivete is often the best defense against 'realistic' predictions for the future. The future has always been known to evade predictions. Rosa Parks didn't know she was participating in the Civil Rights movement when she demanded a seat at the front of the bus.

If we demand a seat at the front of the bus for children now, perhaps they'll one day have the foundation to develop a fully functional Global Peace movement. That can be good for children all over the world, in all ages to come. And that—according to educators and parents on both sides of the paradigm issue—is the purpose of education.

## Integrating the Internet into K-12 Education

Some educators use computers in the classroom just for email. Some use them to begin and moderate full-scale international K-12 projects, while others teleconference regularly. However, among the many and varied educators currently coming into their own with computers in the classroom, most will use it for some level of involvement in between.

In 1995, Microsoft announced the birth of "The Connected Learning Community," a worldwide educational community of students, parents, and educators based upon the Internet. This came at the same time as Microsoft's announced partnership with the Global Schoolhouse, giving new life to one of the most prominent international K-12 educational project, which had recently lost its original NFS funding grant.

According to Microsoft CEO Bill Gates, The Connected Learning Community will be a practical environment connecting schools, homes, and the rest of the world. Within this environment, educators will facilitate learning rather than lead it, and students will be introduced to educational materials from all over the world. This is Gates' vision for the education of the future.

Within that community, it falls to educators to work the Internet into school curriculum in a way that makes the most of the opportunity. The choices are staggering. When you brainstorm on your own curriculum and how the Internet can be used to enhance and illuminate it, keep in mind certain points:

1. **Learn email.** Find another educator to communicate with, and exchange email regularly until it's natural to you. The larger your educational community online, the easier it will be for you to get involved with the Internet. The most important thing about the Internet is not that it provides a plethora of information, but that it brings people together.

This will be especially obvious when you get involved with online educational organizations. There is an enormous community out there already, including such pioneers as Yvonne Marie Andres of the Global Schoolhouse and Odd de Presno of KIDLINK. At this point in time, that community is small enough that you may find yourself chatting with one of the founders of a prominent K-12 organization, as well as giving advice to educators and parents even newer to the Internet than you are.

Unfortunately, as the number of educators online explodes, that will soon end. So make friends now, find your mentors in those who make the most substantial contributions to the organizations you belong to, and build your own personal network of educators and parents who share your interests and challenges; people you can email privately for advice, professional camaraderie, or just commiseration.

By permission of Mike Luckovich and Creators Syndicate

And remember that as soon as you learn something, there will be someone to teach it to. Educators and parents are constantly joining the online community. All it takes is one day, and someone is already following in your footsteps. Be sure to extend a hand to those who need it.

2. **Don't take on too much too quickly.** Start with a small project, something quick and easy, to introduce the idea to your class and, at the same time, build your own confidence. It's better to keep your momentum up than to get in over your head.

Children learn fast. You don't want them getting ahead of you from the start, or your chances of catching up are slim. Take the time to learn the basics thoroughly: email, search engines, bulletin boards. Then, teach them to your class.

For example, take the traditional library model for searching for information as your prototype, and use online search engines to locate specific information. When you're comfortable with it, expand upon the search model to cover more complex material.

Also, consider yourself a perennial student. No one will ever learn all there is to know about computers in the classroom, and even the most experienced educators claim that they work every day to stay one step ahead of their students.

3. **Ask your students for ideas.** Some of their ideas will be trivial and some will be outrageous—as is true of all good brainstorming—but many will be worth investigating. Remember that what they're interested in learning, they'll learn better and retain longer.

As the educational paradigm shifts into the students' arena, children take on more and more responsibility for giving input to their own curriculum. Help them take on this responsibility a little at a time.

You can begin, as always, with something small, like allowing them their own email accounts, and move gradually into more important areas. It's a good exercise to let the most motivated students design and maintain your class's home page on the Web, while asking the rest of the class for input. It's also useful to train your students to participate directly in projects, such as typing in class responses when there are only a few terminals available, rather than relying on your own ability to stay on top of the workload. They'll appreciate the sense of accomplishment, while freeing your time for less menial chores.

A note of caution: students communicating over a network should always be supervised, for their own sake more than the school's. It's the responsibility of all adults involved in children's experiences with the Internet to help keep those experiences safe. Even KIDCAFE, a heavily-monitored international children's chat group, depends upon educators and parents to read incoming mail to all students in order to screen out suspicious or unacceptable mail.

4. **Use your imagination.** The Internet is a largely untapped resource in many ways, and its integration into the K-12 classroom is still in the early phases. The ideas you originate today may become the standards for teachers who follow.

Explore the opportunities. This is how people get addicted to surfing the Web. Once you get an idea of the amount of resources available, you'll be overwhelmed.

Try to stay on top of the brainstorms you have while you're exploring, either by writing them down or by exploring with another educator who can help you keep track of them. Otherwise, you'll find yourself in the same state as Bryant Elementary School Technology Leader Virginia Davis, who cried to her students, "I've got so many ideas I can't stand it!"

Remember that the point is not to collect information for information's sake, but to use the Internet to find information you need for a particular purpose. When you consider a project, ask yourself, "What is the projected outcome? And what can I do with that result?" Often, the answer to this question will give you an idea for a project in the future, and you'll find that your projects build upon each other, lending each one depth and scope.

Also, remember that your enthusiasm is contagious. When you're excited, your students will get excited. What they learn in that adrenaline state will stay with them longer and they'll be inclined to go home and share it with their families, reinforcing their memories.

5. **In designing your own projects, use other educators' ideas to start with and build from there.** Very few teachers mind lending their expertise to others, particularly when it comes to helping you through an introductory time that they have all gone through themselves. If you have any questions about what's appropriate and what's not, feel free to contact the teacher directly. If you don't know who originated an idea, all of the organizations listed under "Resources" are always willing to help.

Many children's Internet projects are short-lived because the outcome is a goal the children look forward to eagerly. However, the examples of the successful short-term projects here can give you an idea of what types of projects work well over the Internet, and they can help you come up with ideas for projects of your own.

One of the most fundamental recent projects over the Internet is KIDLINK's Children's Bill of Rights. In this project, which ran through March and April of

1996, students from all over the world brainstormed on the rights of children and discussed topics relating to children's rights. The topics were introduced by project moderators Lena Rotenberg and Lawry de Bivort of the USA, and the children's discussions were conducted over IRC. The final Bill of Rights is scheduled to be presented for students' approval in the Fall of 1996.

Hopeful Headlines, another KIDLINK project, moderated by Joann Wilson of the USA and Heather Ballantyne of New Zealand, was designed to give children a place to discuss their hopes for the environment. Originally, discussions were held within each class, with the students identifying some local issue that impacted their environment in a particular way. The results of these discussions were posted on the Internet as "community profiles." Students from around the world then wrote headlines, in which the concerns of each other's classes were treated as news, for newspaper stories from the future.

Classroom Connect is a newsletter that focuses directly on the issues of integrating the Internet into the K-12 classroom. The lesson plans, in particular, can be a great help to the online educator. Specified grade levels in the lesson plans are general (such as K-2, 3-5, 9-12), and there are normally three or four objectives to each lesson plan, like learning about a specific science, creating an awareness of culture, and communicating with another class. The necessary materials that are listed with each plan include, at a minimum, a computer connected to the Internet, although often Web access is also required. The lesson plan procedures themselves are described in simple, straightforward steps, including questions for the students to consider and related activities such as making maps.

You can use the steps themselves as a model for projects you create on your own. Remember to keep it simple and fun.

Moderators Indu Varma of Canada and Tor Ane Richvoldsen of Norway recently concluded the project Blue Print Earth, in which students addressed the issues of current environmental problems. Children were encouraged to identify environmental problems and then find new and innovative ways to solve them, whether by writing educational materials, working solutions into proposed political and social schemes, or by creating "gadgets" that made it possible to protect the future of the environment.

Virtual Vacation was a two-time project operated through KILDINK by moderators Mary Esborn of the USA and Mariko Fujita of Japan. Children designed "vacations" in their home cities and countries for children from around the world, in which they first created an itinerary and then described the steps of the itinerary for their "virtual" tourists. Students were able to tour each other's homes and trade questions about their vacations. This project was so popular when it ran in 1993 that it was run again in 1995.

6. **Get involved with established online K-12 organizations, such as those listed under "Resources," and participate in a few group projects before designing your own.** Once you're interested in designing your own projects, consider introducing them to the group. The sense of community you'll get from working with other educators and parents, sharing the same projects and concerns, will carry you through a multitude of frustrations and revelations and will finally be what you take home with you at the end of the day.

7. **Never forget that the point of having computers in the K-12 classroom is to enhance your students' education.** When presented with the choice between two exciting projects, ask yourself, "From which will my students learn more? Which gives them a lesson with greater applicability? Which gives them more opportunities to expand upon that education?"

Resist the impulse to get involved in a project just because it looks impressive. There are far more projects going on right now than you can get your students involved in. You'll have to pick and choose.

Brainstorm with your class at the beginning of the school year on the most important functions of education and create a list. For example:

-  helps us in our daily lives (such as math, reading, cooking, and other practical experiences)

- teaches us about our environment (such as earth sciences)

- shows us a way to improve the world we live in (such as exploring social issues)

- gives us experience in sharing and conflict resolution (such as communication across cultures, discussion groups)

You can also create a list of least important functions, to keep you on track. For example:

- entertains us (such as playing games)

- promotes competitiveness (such as unrealistically-weighted competitions)

- trains us in rote mechanics (such as collecting useless information)

- distracts us (such as Web surfing)

It's not that any particular functions are universally positive or negative. There is a time and a place for nearly every behavior in the human repertoire. However, your focus is on K-12 education, and within the limited time that you and your class have together, you'll have priorities on how to best realize your goals. Clarify those priorities for yourselves and post them somewhere in the classroom for the duration of the school year, and you'll have established guidelines by which to judge your involvement in any projects you consider.

In this way, you can adhere to both your curriculum and your values, and make sure that your students get the best out of their experiences with computers in the classroom.

*"From the mentor in the center to the guide on the side."*

# Case Studies

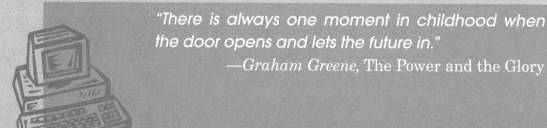

"There is always one moment in childhood when the door opens and lets the future in."

—*Graham Greene*, The Power and the Glory

**D**uring the months of February and March of 1996, I visited three schools in the San Francisco Bay Area—a high school, a middle school, and an elementary school. Each one had a unique student body, a unique background, and a unique perspective on education. However, they all shared one goal: to integrate educational technology into their curriculums.

In addition, on February 3, 1996, Brendan and I attended the second-ever prototype of California's NetDay96, a monumental project that involved wiring 100 classrooms in one day. With the help of numerous volunteers from all aspects of the community, that phototype was a resounding success and it laid the groundwork for Santa Clara's role in the March 9 NetDay96—the wiring of schools throughout California. This was the birth of Silicon Valley's own networked county of schools and of perhaps the largest K-12 network in the world.

Please allow me to introduce you to the people who made that possible, a few of the pioneers on the forefront of educational technology, who hack a path through the jungle today in order to clear the way for the educators of tomorrow.

*Victoria*

## NetDay96, Santa Clara County, California

Oak Grove High School in San Jose, California, has one hundred classrooms. On February 3, 1996, over a month before NetDay96, 230 volunteers assembled in the Oak Grove cafeteria to participate in a prototype of NetDay that was organized by the San Jose Education Network (SJEN) in conjunction with Oak Grove School. Parents, teachers, ex-students, and current students came together to wire the hundred classrooms of Oak Grove for computer access to the Internet.

This was a step away from centralized bureaucratic operation and back to the quilting bee/barn raising paradigm, learning by participating. Once these kids learned how to strip a wire and do the connecting, they'd never forget it. Suddenly, in one Saturday, the children stepped into the technical world.

NetDay96 was announced by President Clinton in 1995 as the implementation of NII, the National Information Infrastructure, in K-12 schools.

NetDay96 was set for March 9 and, on that day, schools across the country planned to hook up for the first time to the Internet.

SJEN is an independent foundation that's responsible for the NetDay96 effort in Santa Clara County. SJEN staged the NetDay prototype at Oak Grove in order to test the waters before NetDay itself arrived.

*Getting Started*

In preparation for their NetDay prototype, Oak Grove High School printed instructions on teams and team assignments, which were already arranged, along with maps of the school campus. After preliminary speeches by SJEN Executive Director David Katz and Oak Grove Principal Karalee Roland, the volunteers were divided into six teams and directed to classrooms for training.

In a typical training session, a technical volunteer from 3-Com addressed two dozen volunteers—two teams—of adults and teenagers, teachers and parents. He explained how to wire the classrooms for regular Ethernet transmission with the capability of going to Fast Ethernet transmission at a later time. He demonstrated how to twist the wires to avoid crosstalk.

Each team was assigned to a building or group of buildings. They were shown the blue wires that hang from the ceiling of each room, where a ceiling tile had been pushed aside, and instructed to pull these wires down and attach them through plastic conduits to the walls.

The volunteers of one team decided that one person would be *materials distributor*, another would go from room to room stripping the wires, and the rest would follow and terminate the wires in plugs, running the lengths of the wires through the conduits. Each team had a walkie-talkie, and every technical volunteer had a student "shadow."

Security, like everything at Oak Grove, was well planned and executed. Each volunteer was given an identification badge. The school grounds were patrolled by student ROTC enlistees who guarded the doorways to all classrooms, monitoring who came and went.

*Technical Maintenance*

SJEN plans to build an organizational infrastructure to help the Santa Clara County schools maintain their educational technology. The problem is that in most schools there may be somebody doing the technical work, but they're not assigned to it, so it's not a priority in their workload. To solve this, SJEN plans to use students to maintain the network within each school, with Novell helping to train high school students as network administrators. David Katz described the student CNAs as SJEN's "21st-century AV crew."

First, SJEN trained twenty-two teachers from those schools, which means they had a certificate exam they needed to pass. Then, the schools trained about twenty kids to serve as an advanced help network—the students report to their site, which reports to the district, which gets advice from Novell. Both 3-Com and Sun participate in this program, too.

The pilot program for student network administrators consisted of ten students from different classes, all freshmen and sophomores, who went through an Information Literacy Program in school. Those who were accepted went into the system administration program. Then SJEN trained them to be CNAs, certified network administrators, through Novell's Industry Standards program.

The SJEN routers are remote office products, so they can be operated at the district office, but schools still need adult technical assistance at the district level and professional support at the school level. David expects to always have adults running the training program and handling district-wide networking.

*Safety*

David believes that the safety of children on the Internet depends upon teachers making their kids informed users of information. To restrict student access is to destroy the model. Teachers have to make their expectations clear to the kids and not enforce control of the technology, but of the kids. It's about responsibility, like any other aspect of education. However, he does expect ratings to go into effect, eventually.

Oak Grove is unique among the schools visited in that the students are old enough to take part in the move toward technology. Jason Wilkins is 16 years old, a junior at Oak Grove, and one of their computer whiz kids. He helped design Oak Grove's Web page.

Jason brings a different perspective to the issue of children's safety on the Internet. He believes that there's a difference between students accidentally stumbling across pornography—or even taking a look once out of curiosity—and abusing the school's resources by visiting pornographic sites regularly. He would like to see something written that logs the number of times something is accessed, so you can base your screening on that.

According to David, the kids love the Santa Clara County move toward educational technology. Some schools train students to tutor their own teachers, which turns out to be a good way to promote the changes in the educational model from teacher-centered to student-centered. In fact, David is still in contact with some kids who went through this program and have since graduated and gone on to college.

When your students are truly excited about an opportunity like educational technology, they're motivated to learn how to handle it responsibly.

*Training
Teachers*

Karalee Roland has pushed her school to the cutting edge of educational technology through determination rather than exceptional funding. Motivating teachers and school administrators to help bring technology into the K-12 classroom is her key strategy.

Sun Microsystems provided her with a NetDay96 video that they made during the NetDay prototype at Piedmont High School, the first San Jose High School to be wired in one of these volunteer work days and the precursor to Oak Grove's prototype. Karalee has used the video to get the administrations of other schools interested in NetDay and in getting their classrooms wired.

David believes that teachers are very receptive to the new technology. The SJEN program started just as teachers were becoming aware of networking power. The first $50,000 of Mayor Susan Hammer's allocation went into a planning grant for schools, in order to encourage them to use the allocation wisely.

However, schools need the internal capacity to train teachers in technical issues, using the teachers' own motivation as well as student help. According to David and Karalee, schools need a tremendous amount of support for the teachers. The gap between available resources and implementation is agonizing. Teachers need help asking questions about being hooked up, such as, "Why *should* do you it? How do you plan for it?" Schools must take an "enlightened" stance. They need to get their teachers ready, train them, get them access to the technology, start budgeting, help them decide where they're going to spend the allotted money first. In particular, schools need to educate teachers on the pressures they will be under, with a clear understanding that they *will* be under pressure.

Teachers need to understand the difference between having access to information and communication. Educational technology is not just about getting information off the Web. Teachers have the ability to network with other teachers all over the world through the Internet.

*Funding*

SJEN started in 1993, when Mayor Hammer set aside $1 million from San Jose City to promote technology in the schools, reflecting her 'vision' of Silicon Valley's influence on the San Jose City's quality of education and life. San Jose has the greatest concentration of computer technology in the world in the Silicon Valley—Mayor Hammer wanted that expertise to benefit the local children and schools.

The districts pay half of the costs of wiring the Santa Clara County schools and of providing teachers with work stations, and SJEN pays the other half. SJEN has raised about $6 million beyond the mayor's original $1 million, so far. David manages the fund-raising and organizes the summer training for teachers. He brokers discounts, donations, and volunteers.

The SJEN plans for NetDay were more strict than statewide plans. SJEN required each school to submit a comprehensive written plan that met SJEN standards and a commitment from the school to pay for whatever SJEN couldn't.

According to David, the smartest thing SJEN did was make the schools commit to using the limited resources they already had, setting up their networks, before SJEN committed to helping them. Schools need corporations and training institutions in order to build a real community. David believes that the single most unanimously held value in our society is a good education. In his experience as a fundraiser, if you build commitment, dollars follow.

*The Future*

San Jose's participation in the March 9th NetDay96, was a huge success. SJEN wired 102 schools in Santa Clara County with the help of approximately 8,000 volunteers. Many of the schools were wired on March 9 itself, and the day was very similar to Oak Grove's prototype.

SJEN started in 1993 with one networked school. After NetDay96, 71 percent of the schools in Santa Clara County had routed Internet connections, and 42 percent—two-thirds of those—were completely wired. Out of 335 schools in 34 districts countywide, SJEN only had one or two high schools left to do. The rest of the schools, the other 29 percent, are middle and elementary schools, and David expects to have those finished within eighteen months. When it's finished, Santa Clara County will have the largest county-wide K-12 network in the world.

## Oak Grove High School, San Jose, California

Greg Barnett is a teacher of English as a Second Language at Oak Grove High School. Greg has three computers in his classroom: two on a long table in a front corner and one on his desk. Greg was heavily involved in the NetDay96 prototype conducted at Oak Grove and was the first teacher to get his computers online.

Time is the big issue at Oak Grove, where training programs are still being developed, funds being acquired, and many of the teachers are too busy to learn a new—and complicated—tool like computer technology.

*Getting Started*

Greg stayed late on NetDay and did a lot of the wiring work himself. According to Greg, the school didn't have a lot of the components out of storage yet that day and the district engineer still needed to put the cards into most of the computers. His point was that getting a school online takes time.

Greg spent around thirty hours in the month before the NetDay prototype working after school hours on the network with the Oak Grove technical coordinator Greg Brazil. They created a "share file" so that, when other teachers get their computers hooked up, they can transfer the necessary ShareWare off Greg Barnett's computer instead of having to find it on the Web and download it. This type of free software is extremely valuable to a school with limited funding. In addition, Greg Barnett wants to purchase a TV for his classroom, and Principal Karalee Roland agrees that unless you have a computer for everyone, you've got to get the computer screen onto television.

*Technical Maintenance*

Oak Grove has a Technical Staff Development group of thirty teachers. The members of this group have gone through the San Jose Education Network training. Oak Grove produced a flyer titled, "Network Ethics and Computer Technology Usage Agreement," and the group went through the booklet, signed the AUP form, and discussed the issues among themselves. Karalee hoped to be able to provide them with some time to work on the Internet, but she didn't expect them to gain a tremendous amount of skill on the Internet in a two-hour workshop, when some of them don't have a computer back in their classroom to practice on.

In addition, Karalee sent Greg Barnett, along with Greg Brazil and another teacher, to a three-day consortium offered by the Santa Clara County Office. The County solicited three teachers from each school for a consortium to help educators integrate the Internet into their curriculum, asking that the schools send teachers who already had Internet skills.

When Greg Barnett and the others returned from the workshop, they brought what they learned back to the school and trained the other teachers. In this way, teachers saw how they could successfully use the Internet in their curriculum.

*Safety*

Karalee is concerned about the safety of children on the Internet. She believes that students must be guided.

It is not acceptable for students to use Oak Grove computers to look for sexual material on the Internet. The students must understand the Acceptable Use Policy that they sign, and they must understand what they're doing when they're online. She agreed that having teachers monitor the students is also essential, but the two methods go hand-in-hand. Even in a smaller class, as few as twenty-five students, if a teacher has ten kids on the computers and fifteen working at their desks, the teacher can't monitor everything everyone's doing. The Oak Grove computers are all over campus—in the library and the Administration Building, as well as the classrooms— and it's difficult to keep track of who's where.

Possible inappropriate contact from adults is also an issue. The number of teachers who know how to handle abuse must increase. It won't be a counselor who hears about such contact first, but a classroom teacher. Some teachers aren't comfortable dealing with the problem directly, in which case the school needs to provide them with the proper steps and procedures that allow someone else to take over. Some teachers feel comfortable dealing with the problem directly, but still don't know the proper steps to take. All teachers will have to expand their awareness of abuse beyond mandatory reporting.

*Training Teachers*

Oak Grove, more than some other schools, seems to be struggling with resistance to educational technology among the faculty. Karalee does not believe in making technology mandatory in the classroom. It's better to work around those individuals who don't want to learn about computers than to hold up the whole process. There's enough to do without wasting energy on struggling to mandate educational technology.

It's hard to introduce computers as a tool, because there is such a degree of sophistication to it. Teachers may need to educate themselves on this sophisticated tool and may not necessarily have the time.

Karalee recommends not locking horns with teachers who resist educational technology in the K-12 classroom. She sees two motivations behind their resistance: control issues and fear. She expects all of her teachers to be interested in the Internet in the long run, once they've seen how it works in other classrooms.

Some of the Oak Grove teachers have begun to learn programs for their own personal management tools, and Karalee hopes this is the first step toward accepting technology in the classroom. If the teachers use some type of software, they get interested in learning about more resources.

However, until the schools have more people like Greg Barnett, who have been creative with using the Internet in the classroom and who have done the work of learning about it, making the transition to educational technology will be difficult. Greg is confronted frequently with the problem of teaching less-technical teachers about computers. According to Karalee, the problem is the faculty's awareness of technology and their understanding of technical issues. Greg wants to learn "everything" because it helps his students, so he winds up helping other teachers because he can. Until that attitude permeates the schools, Karalee predicted, the schools are going to have trouble.

The answer is "time," Greg said philosophically, "like anything else."

*Resources*          Although neither Greg nor Karalee knew much at the time of the visit about the variety of K-12 resources available through the Internet, Greg did plan to use the Web in his curriculum and to set up an Oak Grove home page.

After the NetDay prototype, Greg stayed after class every day to research the Web. He teaches language acquisition through content, and one of the resources he found on the Internet is a link to the University of Washington, where they have lesson plans and studies on ESL students and how to get students integrated into language through content.

Greg planned to put information on language acquisition versus language learning on his class's home page, so that Web browsers could see the difference between learning Spanish as a foreign language and how his students acquire language through content. He and the other ESL teacher had done some word processing on the computers, but until the NetDay prototype they had done nothing on the Internet.

Greg once taught a course on weather systems, in which he used the Internet to capture screen shots of weather maps so his students could map out the progress of storms, calculate the rates of travel, and make predictions about where the storms would wind up. Eventually, the class could say, 'Hey, it's going to be raining right around the time we go home. Who wants to borrow an umbrella?' And they'd be right.

Greg's goal is to get the students hooked up to their own countries and to libraries in their own languages. That way, when the students do research on a project they can get the information first and translate it into English. Greg uses both email and the Web in his class, and he encourages students who have email addresses for relatives in their native countries to share their expertise with the rest of the students.

In addition, the students know the URL for the Vietnam Pictures Archive at Sunsite, one of their favorite sites. The site contains ordinary pictures of daily life in Vietnam: women selling vegetables at the market, kids playing in water with the water buffalo. These are things the Vietnamese students miss about home. They stand around the computer in the morning and tease each other with normal adolescent patter: 'That's your mom,' pointing at one of the women selling vegetables, or arguing over whose girlfriend the girl in the beautiful white dress is. This is what Greg wants for his students, this contact with their countries and their own cultures. He hopes that it helps alleviate their homesickness.

Greg's students, who speak very little English, did not understand at first that their class had been wired for the Internet. In the week after the NetDay prototype, only one boy was able to describe the Internet, calling it "international," "around the world," and "news." The students were interested, however, in using the Internet to make contact with their native countries: Mexico, the Philippines, Hong Kong, Vietnam, India, and Samoa.

Within a few weeks, they were on the Web researching a unit on animals around the world, each student taking a turn at one of the computers. Although only weeks before they hadn't known what the Internet was, now most of them had enough skill with the mouse and search engines to explore the Web.

*Funding*

Karalee doesn't have the dollars to put a computer in every room, but she wishes she did. Fortunately, the community around Oak Grove made a tremendous effort to bring educational technology to the school even without full funding.

Greg was overwhelmed by the community support Oak Grove received for the NetDay prototype. He had been on a team for two years getting ready to wire the school and, at first, the team felt they'd be lucky to get fifty volunteers from the community to help. The final number wound up being over two hundred.

Greg has former students who are now in the computer field who heard about the NetDay prototype and called to offer their help. Some just walked in and said, "I want to help." Also, some of Greg's former ESL students who had gone on to ESL 3 or who had mainstreamed into regular English classes were there to work on his building.

Greg described it as former students coming back to help the teacher hook up new students, a strong sense of community between students who don't know each other.

*Acceptable
Use Policies*

Karalee believes that the major impact of educational technology on our schools is the moral and ethical issues about being online, for kids and parents as well as the staff.

By NetDay96, Oak Grove's biggest problem with educational technology was plagiarism. The students had figured out where student reports are published online and were turning in entire projects done by students across the country. In the past, students haven't had full reports supplied to them in this way. They may have been able to lift a paragraph here or there, but those were written by professionals, and the difference in style was usually apparent to any English teacher. Now Greg and Karalee may begin checking with the parents to find out if the child did the homework when they suspect a student didn't write the report. It may be feasible for more of the homework to be done in the classroom, so the teacher can at least make sure it's getting started, but there is a limit.

Perhaps unfortunately, there's so much available online that it's almost impossible to control. Karalee wants the students to simply learn that when they cheat on homework they cheat themselves.

*The Future*

Karalee expects to see educational technology being used as a tool much more within the next five years than it currently is. She also thinks that the students will be the experts.

Teachers will be facilitators or collaborators. While Oak Grove currently had some teachers who believe they're lowering their standards by bringing technology into the classroom, Karalee hopes they can move over for progress. She's sure that younger teachers will be able to handle this new educational model.

Beyond technical or even funding problems, most educators say the shift in the educational paradigm will be the biggest obstacle to educational technology, and Karalee agrees. Safety, morality, and ethics, she said: those are going to be the toughies.

# Berkeley Montesorri Middle School
# Berkeley, California

There are two aspects to Montesorri education: from one, the children are taught how to work within their group and to deal with cultural tools, and from the other, educators create a process by which children are given their tools and skills on several levels, including emotional, social, physical, and cognitive. According to Berkeley Montesorri School Director Curt Chamberlain, the computer is about information, and as an information tool it's important to teach the children to use it.

Montesorri puts the computer into a category of cultural tools called Practical Life. Brooms are for sweeping, and sponges are for cleaning, and computers also perform certain functions. Middle School Director Lynne Miles stressed that there's nothing mystifying or deifying about it. Computers are just there.

*Getting Started*

Berkeley Montesorri's original computer was an Apple II that was so slow Lynne could get up and walk around the room while it was processing. That was ten years ago. Now, they have PowerMacs and are connecting to the Internet.

Curt and Lynne haven't been on the Internet much yet, and they are still considering whether or not to have the ISDN lines put into the building, because they may move within the next few years.

Curt and Lynne don't have problems with parents objecting to computers in the classroom, although Curt said that they do get some "quirky" people in Berkeley. The harder ones to handle are the "super-techies," who want a lot of technology at the K-12 level. Some parents of pre-kindergarten children want educational technology in the pre-K classroom. Some parents simply want to be able to say, "We have computers in our child's class!"

Curt tries to balance that out, asking himself, "Of what use is this to the children's development?" For instance, the minicomputer training course for kindergarten kids that the school offers is sensory rather than concrete. Curt explains the school's philosophies and goals to parents who ask for more technology, outlining the balance between the different development areas that Montesorri addresses, and he finds that they appreciate that.

Middle School teacher Rebecca Pevsner manages educational technology at Berkeley Montesorri. She learned Fortran programming in college and, since then, has taken educational technology workshops from California State University and from a Berkeley women's organization, among others. She feels particularly lucky to be an educator with several years of experience with technology and with contacts in the industry. She has close friends at Apple and Microsoft, and when she first got involved in the computers in the classroom, she called them up and said, "What do I do?" and they said, "This is how you do it. This is where you start."

Her friends recommended that she go to the Mac Expo, a yearly conference for Macintosh enthusiasts. That's where she got her first software, references, and advice in launching the Berkeley Montesorri educational technology program.

*Technical*
*Maintenance*

Berkeley Montesorri has a computer specialist whom they pay to do system administration work: a parent and member of the administration staff. It's turned out to be very useful to have a mentor for the school, particularly for the teachers. When Curt has a question he calls their mentor, and the mentor can usually come into the classroom and say, "This is the problem."

In addition to the technical mentor, Berkeley Montesorri has a freelance computer teacher come in twice a week to work with the students. Stuart Reiter teaches at Berkeley Montesorri on Mondays and Tuesdays, one hour each day in the Middle School and one in the Upper Elementary School. Stuart teaches computer science professionally to both children and adults. His slogan is, "Getting Rid of Fear."

According to Rebecca, each school needs a technology point person to coordinate teacher training. You need one of these technical people for every school because the Internet is always changing, "it's an organic technical growth." She would like each school to have someone they can send to lots of workshops, someone for whom the school rents a computer if they don't have one at home. This technical contact must be able to troubleshoot, but must also be a teacher, someone who can do planning and handle funding.

You need someone who can make global decisions, like, "Are we going to network? How are we going to do it? Do we want a lab? Will the technology we use serve our curriculum needs?"

You need someone who can tell parents, "Being good at video games is not the same thing as having computer skills."

You need someone to screen the software and decide about appropriate in-house use. Berkeley Montesorri gets a lot of parents donating software, and Rebecca screens every single piece of it that comes into this school. She sends a lot of it back as incompatible with Montesorri goals.

You need a person who is the school touchstone, who gets funded to be the touchstone.

*Safety*

Montesorri emphasizes group process work about responsibility and making wise choices. There are rules that the school teaches as a part of being responsible, like not giving out your phone number or your credit card number. Berkeley Montesorri tries to address things like how students should handle homeless people asking for money on the streets and teaches them to be more aware of their surroundings.

When confronted with the issue of children's safety on the Internet, Lynne referred to an article she'd read recently, in which adults are encouraged to talk to the children about what's out there, what they may come across, and tell them that if they see anything questionable they should just ask for help. Lynne tells the children "There are going to be some weird people out there." She believes that the risk in Berkeley is greater just going down the street to the grocery story.

Berkeley Montesorri will probably write permission forms for parents to sign. Lynne paraphrases it as, "Your child will be on the Internet. Do we have your permission to let them venture into cyberspace? There are risks, but we will do our best to maintain watchfulness."

According to Rebecca, the fact is that there are people out there who mean nothing but harm, and she wants her kids to know that so they're prepared. Rebecca has done adolescent development, answering anonymous questions about sexuality, and she found that answering questions like that can be hard. In some cases, a teacher might have to make mandatory reports. However, she feels strongly that you *must* answer such questions.

In addition to the safety of the kids, Rebecca is concerned about advertising and marketing. She pointed out that it did not take very long for the Home Shopping Network to get online, and said that she may be philosophically against censorship of the Internet, but realistically there are some still things she would be happy to censor. She discusses this paradox with her middle school students and finds that they're at a great age for discussions.

The whole thrust of Montesorri education is empowering children so they make wise choices. Adults can't always be around to protect the students, so the students have to be able to protect themselves.

Addressing abuse and the potential for it and how students should handle it if someone tries it with them—that needs to be interwoven with your regular curriculum. You must be very aware of what's going on. You must prepare the kids. You must work with each child to create the strongest, most whole person that you can.

*Training*
*Teachers*

Teachers need both training and support. However, it's often the children who learn faster and become the helpers—especially those children whose parents have computer experience. At the time of the visit, Berkeley Montesorri depended heavily upon Rebecca. She was the motivating force behind training the Berkeley Montesorri teachers.

Rebecca had seen friends of hers who are teachers get into technology over their heads, using the example of someone who wants to make videos, but only finds out later that video takes too much memory so they can't save their kids' projects. You can get into situations where you're not helping the kids. Projects on the Internet can easily balloon, especially in terms of time management.

The Montesorri approach involves not only addressing the issue of computers in society, but also using the computer to develop children's skills. It has to do with the fact that when you're typing at a keyboard with both hands, you're using both hemispheres of your brain. While the fine motor skills involved in typing and using a mouse develop at around the age of six, many children who have difficulty with tasks like revision and organization do much better on a computer, where both the linear and conceptual parts of the brain are stimulated simultaneously.

Unfortunately, few teachers have access to a computer for each of their students. If you only get one computer, you can do cooperative work, using a big sheet of paper on the wall to assign a role to each student on each day. Rebecca pointed out that you can do this type of cooperative work without computers.

Rebecca has trained every elementary school teacher at Berkeley Montesorri to be comfortable on the machines, even though there are some who may say they only know because Rebecca made them learn it. The first threshold to educational technology is showing teachers what technology is.

Sometimes you just have to articulate to teachers who are new to technology that it's okay not to jump into it all at once. Once you've been trained, Rebecca said, you can be fine with letting the kids lead you because you have the basic framework.

Rebecca also feels that it's important to address the issue of teachers' reluctance to bring computers into the classroom. She feels that her girls' reluctance to assert themselves in getting time on the computer is similar to the teachers' reluctance. Many of the teachers that she's worked with have said they were afraid they'd make a mistake or break the computer. Rebecca tells them she'll show them how not to break it.

The school's technical coordinator can work with the teachers to show them how the computer empowers them, and once the teachers learn something like ClarisWorks, it frees up their time. Rebecca can understand a teacher who barely can afford chalk looking at computers and saying, "Aaaaaagh!"

When Berkeley Montesorri first started, Lynne was involved in teaching the children word processing and even programming, in which they learned concepts like recursion. Lynne remembered that as being fun and described it as "the fun beginning!"

At the time of the visit, Berkeley Montesorri's educational technology program had moved into Stuart's domain. According to Stuart, public schools have no one to teach computer classes, because you can't get accredited to teach computers without 20 to 40 credits of Computer Science. Stuart doesn't understand who would to do that and then go into teaching for $30,000 a year, so he's waiting to see what kind of educational opportunities develop in the next five years.

Stuart and Rebecca meet regularly to set up a Computer Science unit around a particular set of ideas for the kids. Because they have to rotate the students on the four computers, it takes three or four weeks to go through each set of ideas.

In teaching four Middle School students for an hour each day, Stuart maintains a five-way dialogue for forty minutes, remaining calm and thoughtful throughout. Some students ricochet between elation and annoyance over the opportunities and limits of their computer programs. Some students are already experienced computer users, like Richard, who called on his own initiative and arranged for Berkeley Montesorri to buy their four copies of *The Incredible Machine*, a tool for cognitive skills. Some students are new to educational technology and remain absorbed in each puzzle as it comes along.

*Resources*

What Berkeley Montesorri does not want to use computer for is any kind of drill, which means they don't use software that has to do with reading and math. They do like all the simulation programs, like Carmen Sandiego, and are now trying to get into more sophisticated software such as video and scanners.

Lynne has immediate reservations about any programs that are solely animation. In Montesorri, one of the most important things to address, particularly at an early age, is focus and concentration. The difference is between reading a book, in which you envision the characters and the story and you project your own imagination into it, and having a story fed to you by an activated screen. The more hours children spend being fed stories, the less active their imaginations are. Lynne equates animation programs with television, saying that she strongly resists animated games for the same reason.

Their goal is to thoroughly integrate the computer into the classroom, so the students go to the computers for assignments that computers specifically address, like word processing and research. Lynne gave the example of a unit they were currently teaching about China. In typical Montesorri fashion, the class covered history, literature, and geography, rather than the traditional segregated approach. The school's plan was to produce a part of that unit's curriculum that dealt with research, for which the students could use the Internet.

Rebecca called her first year online "the year of leveling the playing field." She wanted all the kids in the Middle School to have equal skills by the end of the year. She focused on word processing, graphics, and simple self-publishing, calling self-publishing a wonderful tool, "all about having ideas and getting them out there." She's also done typing assessments, taught the students spreadsheets and data charts, and taught them to wrap text around images.

Equality is important to Rebecca, in her world view, as well as her focus on education. Although she's very aware of ways in which the Internet creates inequality, she has hopes for using it to build equality, too. She planned a two-year mentoring project with the author Teri Perl, in which they'd connect adolescent girls to women in the sciences for real time chats over the Internet.

Some of Rebecca's favorite software is *Sunburst Wings for Learning*, *Adam Essentials*, and *Measuring Emotion* as having excellent links to curriculum. She uses *KID PIX* and *Dabbler* and can't say enough in favor of them. She's used the *Math Bundles* for grades 5-8, from the Apple Education Series, with probability constructors, and next year will do the section on *Movement in Motion*, which is physics.

At the time of the visit, she was using *The Incredible Machine* and was very enthusiastic about it. She has also used *Myst* for the upper elementary kids, 4th and 5th grades.

Rebecca established steps toward getting the Internet fully involved in her curriculum: teaching spreadsheets and databases, tabulating information, free drawing, assessing cut and paste skills, teaching students to wrap text around images, cognitive work, and introduction to the Internet. At that point, her class was almost all the way through the steps. The next thing she planned was an Internet workshop in order for everyone to gain "facility" on the computers. Rebecca filled up her bookmarks section and had the students work in pairs gathering information.

One common goal in Montesorri is for kids to become specialists. In this unit, each student would be a specialist in something and would train others in their specialty. Then they'd present it in newspaper format—with editorials, news, and an article on cooking. Rebecca would print one copy of the newspaper in color for the whole class and individual black and white copies for the students.

Rebecca sees a great distinction between collecting information and presenting it, and that's what she wants to address with educational technology: the transformative step in between.

*Funding*

Berkeley Montesorri operates on foundation money, meaning grants. They always go out looking for support and expect eventually to budget a regular salary for a technical mentor.

Berkeley Montesorri purchases all of their computer hardware, including the PowerMacs. Although they do get fixer-upper donations, they'd rather buy new machines than invest in repairs.

*Acceptable Use Policies*

Your school's technical contact can also be assigned to write your Acceptable Use Policy. Rebecca wrote the AUP for Berkeley Montesorri, but said that she basically just added their specifics to a copy of an online one that she downloaded from Lake Wolmerdink School. Lake Wolmerdink is north of Berkeley in the Richmond/Martinez area, and she considers the work they do cutting edge.

Rebecca pointed out a quote by Odvard Egil Dyrli, Professor Emeritus at the University of Connecticut: "Acceptable Use Policies change the focus from external to internal control." Rebecca believes that AUPs are about responsibility. The Internet works with Montesorri because it's a self-directed tool, and she tells the kids that—it's only a tool. It will not do their work for them.

*The Future*

Rebecca's vision for the future of technology in the classroom is modeled on a Montesorri school in Houston that does an Internet exchange with the Mexico City Montesorri school. The Houston school was two years into the project, running both live video and email.

If the schools get underprivileged kids online, those students can reach out, even in other languages, and they can pull down images and have realtime conversations with people from other countries.

Rebecca is fascinated with the idea of the global village, which is why she was strict in her decision to wait to go online. She wanted to teach the students to handle contact with other cultures with understanding and tolerance.

She doesn't believe that "cooperative learning" would have become such a catchword in a powerful industry like computers if it wasn't working.

Lynne wants to teach the students to appreciate current public debate on the issue of children on the Internet, especially in U.S. Congress, and the widespread discussion going on at this *very moment* about what kinds of protections are appropriate for the

Internet. Issues like civil liberties and free speech are very pertinent to her students, particularly to the teenagers, who love the concepts of freedom and responsibility.

# Bryant Elementary School
# San Francisco, California

Virginia Davis has been the Technology Resources Teacher at Bryant School for eleven years. Everything Virginia knows about networking and computers she's learned in the lab as she went along. Now she is an expert on computer networking in the K-12 classroom and has recently appeared on CNN demonstrating SurfWatch.[1] Her computer lab is considered a model for other schools, and she receives phone calls from all over the world asking her how she built it and how others can do the same.

*Getting*
*Started*

Virginia took the Bryant computer lab from a collection of eight Apple IIe computers to a full Novell network of 34 machines—both old Apples and brand-new Pentiums.

In addition to the computer lab, each classroom at Bryant has four or five computers, all networked on Baseband, Token Ring, and Ethernet, and running off one file server. She has a Ciskei router and six ISDN lines, which give her the ability to send video and sound, and therefore to teleconference with other schools.

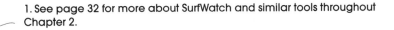

1. See page 32 for more about SurfWatch and similar tools throughout Chapter 2.

Pacific Bell donates the expertise of their school program coordinator to Bryant Elementary, which is one of Pacific Bell's dozen model schools in California. In addition, the San Francisco Exploratorium established an online link with Bryant to bring the Exploratorium's resources to the school, and Bryant acquired a link to the Smithsonian in Washington, D.C.

Virginia designed her network so that Bryant teachers don't have to depend upon having computers in each classroom. The lab allows students to work on papers or projects lab as a group, and spares the teacher the organizational problems of rotating young students on classroom computers. The few classroom computers are used only for special cases, such as students who miss class on lab day or who need extra time to finish their projects.

According to Bryant principal Anastasia Zita, 85 of the 119 schools in San Francisco planned to participate in NetDay96, 40 of which would do the networking on NetDay itself (the rest had already finished networking their schools). Virginia had already networked the Bryant School lab to the classrooms, so all she planned for NetDay was to run a line from her router to the Child Care Center downstairs and set up three computers there for demonstration.

Bryant is the third school Anastasia has worked with on a technology plan. She plans teacher training for the school district and determines the outcomes for the telecommunications section.

### Safety

Virginia has no problems keeping her students safe on the Internet because they're too young to do much exploring. She uses SurfWatch, and that, along with the teacher always being able to see what's going on, works quite well.

Virginia had CNN come into the lab to film her demonstrating SurfWatch. She showed them that when she typed the word "sex" into the search engine, Surf-Watch blocked it. Then someone said, "What about an actual URL?" and typed "http://www.playboy.com" and the Playboy page came up on the screen. Virginia typed "playboy" into the search engine, and sure enough, SurfWatch blocked it. Fortunately, her students are too young to know about URLs.

Virginia also has no problem with the idea of the school censoring what's available to the children online. In the same sense that she wouldn't put Playboy or pornography in her library, she feels responsible for controlling what the children access through the computers. We are the educators. We *are* responsible for managing this material.

*Training Teachers*

Along with maintaining the computer network, Virginia is responsible for staff training on the computers. At Bryant School, 85 percent of the teachers have taught only one to three years. Many of the older teachers left recently on Governor Wilson's Golden Handshake Retirement plan.

Since the teachers at Bryant are all at different levels, Virginia trains them individually. There are two essentials that she recommends teaching to new educators: how students learn, and curriculum. Once teachers have this background, they can integrate computers into their curriculum specifically to build on the students' learning skills.

She has teachers make an agenda for their classes, describing how they plan to use the computers to support their classroom curriculum. This includes a lesson plan and outlines of what software they plan to use. Then she discusses this agenda with the teacher, describing how they can build on the opportunities of the classroom the way she builds on their own knowledge of teaching.

She tries to give each teacher a general overview of the school's computer network and allows the teacher to follow her for a day, observing what she does and discussing their perspective on computers in the K-12 classroom with her. She emphasizes the importance of getting teachers interested on a personal level.

Virginia also teaches multimedia authoring to the Bryant teachers. She has them keep notebooks on what they learn and gives them copies of information sheets of whatever helpful material she's accumulated over the years. She is not just training the teachers on how to use the computers and the Internet, but on how to use the computer lab to teach. She listed the three elements of lessons plans—goal, content, and curriculum—and explained that computers are meant to support what you're teaching.

Virginia draws a distinction between the computer as a new program introduced to the classroom and as a new tool. The computer is a tool, not a lesson in itself. She doesn't teach computers, just as teachers don't teach using blackboards and chalk.

Virginia is philosophical about teachers who simply don't want computers in the K-12 class. A new program comes out every year: Back to Basics, Whole Learning, Developmentally Appropriate Practices, each one supposed to be the fix-all. After a while teachers start seeing old programs come around with new labels. This is why a lot of the teachers who resist computers in the classroom are the ones who have been around the longest. They don't want to be retrained in something that's common teaching practice. According to Virginia, the curriculum itself doesn't change much; how students learn doesn't change much.

She sees these teachers as the ones staying back and keeping the home fires burning. What they do is just as important as what she does. The early pioneers had an established world in the East, a place to send their letters back to. On the other hand, some of the younger teachers come right out of college with a knowledge of computers but no practical experience at applying computers to classroom teaching. Virginia sees them getting high on the computers and losing sight of their objectives for the kids. One teacher tried to teach a first-grade class to make a videotape. Virginia doesn't believe that six-year-olds need to know how to videotape. You have to draw a line.

One of the main issues in getting children involved with computers is management. Virginia set up learning stations around the walls of her Productivity Resource Center so an adult can stand in the middle of the room and see over everyone's shoulder. This way, she knows who's doing all right on their own and who needs help.

The teacher must give the children skills to search for resources themselves so they can use those skills on the Internet. The idea is not just to use the Internet, but to access the Internet to find the information you need to follow the goals of your lesson plan. Teachers who are curriculum-grounded make it easier to find hooks in the content. This makes it easier to manage the children because they're focused. And it's essential to focus on the subject, not the process.

The first step is to teach the teachers to use email. That way, you can network with other teachers. When your first contact with the Internet is other teachers, the rest of your education in telecommunications is rooted in that community.

*Resources*

Virginia has about sixty children's CDs. Microsoft donated a box, and the Multimedia Expo gives the kids CDs. She keeps the books related to the CDs beside each computer. When a student notices a book and says, "Look! They wrote a book about it!" she tells them that, actually, the CD was made out of the book, and if you look on the back you can see there are more books about these characters in the library. And off they go to the school library to find the new books.

In a package of IBM materials, Virginia found a manual on multimedia authoring, IBM LinkWay. Here was something that she could apply to her classroom without losing the interactive elements she finds so important to learning.

For example, Virginia recently ran an interactive project between a group of her students and a PBS Ghostwriter in New York. A scriptwriter explained the elements of a mystery to the children and then, along with their partner school in Mendicino, California, the Bryant children wrote a mystery and sent it back to New York. They were eventually able to interview one of the PBS actors who performs in mysteries.

You don't want the children to fall behind and not know that these tools are available. You want the kids to know there are many different ways to get information, and you want them skilled in applying that knowledge when they need to. A computer is just a new type of resource. In using the Web, Virginia doesn't intend the teachers to simply search for information for the children or to find resources for them, but to define resources to the children and then teach them searching skills along the traditional library model.

Virginia was making plans for the Bryant School Web sites. She kept sketches for her Web site on the Resource Center blackboard showing links to a site for each classroom, which allowed each teacher to manage their own class site.

She took the "higher-potential" children in the third, fourth, and fifth grade classrooms and made them Webmasters of their sites. She showed them how to use Web66 to find other schools' home pages and get ideas on what to do with their own.[2]

She wants the children to use the Web to link to particular subjects and to keep the emphasis on that subject, not on the process of surfing the Web.

There were plenty of projects at Bryant Elementary that the children might want to post on the school's home page. In the Conflict Management project, teams of children wearing special, over-sized turquoise T-shirts and carrying florescent pink clipboards help other children work out their differences. In the Safety Patrol, a group of children tour the side-

2. You can learn more about Web66 on page 77.

walks around Bryant School in the morning and afternoon making sure the kids walk safely across the street, a direct response to a recent accident in which a student was hit by a car.

According to Virginia, using computers in the classroom is about interactivity. Her kids email each other and their partner school in Mendicino. The teachers manage videoconferencing and email. The Bryant Web page allows schools all over the world to learn about Bryant school and to establish contact between Bryant and themselves.

*Funding*

Bryant School has received no donations of computer hardware. Over the years, Virginia has worked with several Bryant School principals to finance the computer lab.

When Virginia started, the current principal was interested in technology and wanted to focus on teaching language skills through technology. They began by using skill-based learning, the Integrated Learning Systems (ILS), which had a management system built into it so the children could progress at their own speed. However, Virginia became frustrated. She saw the computers driving the students instead of the students driving the computers.

In the beginning, Bryant School used their compensatory funding (such as Title I funding) and special program money to purchase computers on a five-year plan. Virginia calls it "creative funding." When IBM saw what Virginia was doing, they donated software and made Bryant School a pilot site.

Low-cost networking computers are expected to be available in the near future, including one from Oracle for as low as $500. Parents are already talking to Anastasia about them, asking if they can be brought right into the school.

The price makes all the difference. According to Anastasia, with that technology available, teachers can do things nobody's dreamed of yet. Those computers will revolutionize education.

*The Future*

When Virginia's students first started teleconferencing, they mostly noticed the differences between themselves and the other kids.

Then one day they initiated a session and the other class was gone, there was no one to talk to. The kids said, "Look! They put their chairs up on their tables just like we do!" Suddenly, it was the similarities they noticed instead of the differences.

The student's welfare is the foundation on which we build everything else. The Internet is a part of that. Teachers like Virginia are changing the way children relate to cultures besides their own. Kids, seeing the ways in which they are like children from other places, making that connection between themselves and others—to Virginia, the value of that cannot be measured.

*"I'm a jungle hacker."*

—*Greg Barnett*, Oak Grove High School

# Conclusion

**A**s children enter the 21st century, the challenges and opportunities they will encounter are virtually limitless. By introducing them to what many feel is the future of communications, kids are given the basic tools they will need to succeed in a variety of settings.

We hope that this book has helped clear some of the fog that surrounds the use and integration of this new medium. You are encouraged to sit down with your kids—whether at home or in your classroom—and discover the Internet's possibilities together.

If you would like to make comments, cite corrections, or find out about later updates of this book, send email to the address

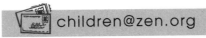 children@zen.org

By permission of Mike Luckovich and Creators Syndicate

 *"The real voyage of discovery consists not in seeking new landscapes, but in having new eyes."*

— *Marcel Proust*

# Available Resources

**T**rying to remember the URLs and FTP sites for the vast expanse of the Internet's offerings can be intimidating. Below are the various Web pages and other sites that were noted throughout this book. We hope that by gathering them together in one place, we'll help speed up your exploration and use of the Net.

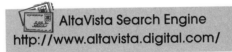

AltaVista Search Engine
http://www.altavista.digital.com/

AskERIC
http://ericir.syr.edu/

AUP templates and legal analysis
http://www.erehwon.com/k12aup/

 Cisco Education Program Grants
http://sunsite.unc.edu/cisco/grant.html

 Classroom Connect
http://www.classroom.net/

 CoSN
http://www.cosn.org/

 White Pine Software CU-SeeMe Clients
http://www.cu-seeme.com/

 Free CU-SeeMe Clients
ftp://gated.cornell.edu/pub/CU-SeeMe/

 CyberPatrol
http://www.cyberpatrol.com/

 CYBERSitter
http://www.solidoak.com/cysitter.htm

 GENII
http://139.132.40.31/GENII/GENIIHP.html

Global Schoolhouse/Global SchoolNet
http://www.gsn.org/

 Global SchoolNet AUPs
http://www.gsn.org/web/issues/aup/home.html

 ICONNECT
http://ericir.syr.edu/ICONN/ihome.html

 IITA
http://quest.arc.nasa.gov/

 InterGO
http://www.teachersoft.com/

 Internet Engineering Task Force (IETF)
http://www.ietf.org/

 Internet Filter
http://www.xmission.com/~seer/jdksoftware/netfilt.html

 iscreen!
http://www.netview.com/

 ISTE
http://isteonline.uoregon.edu/

KIDLINK
http://www.kidlink.org/

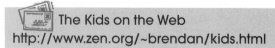
The Kids on the Web
http://www.zen.org/~brendan/kids.html

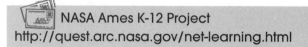
NASA Ames K-12 Project
http://quest.arc.nasa.gov/net-learning.html

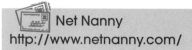
Net Nanny
http://www.netnanny.com/

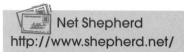
Net Shepherd
http://www.shepherd.net/

NIE
http://www.cise.nsf.gov/cise/ncri/

SafeSurf and PICS
http://www.safesurf.com/

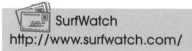
SurfWatch
http://www.surfwatch.com/

TIIAP
http://www.ntia.doc.gov/tiiap/

U.S. Department of Education
http://www.ed.gov/

 Virtual Schoolhouse
http://sunsite.unc.edu/cisco/index.html

 Web66
http://web66.coled.umn.edu/

 Yahoo Search Engine
http://www.yahoo.com/

# Acceptable Use Policies

"Progress imposes not only new possibilities for the future, but new restrictions."
—*Norbet Wiener, The Human Use of Human Beings*

**O**ne of the fundamental aspects of a school being connected to the Internet is setting some base rules that everyone must follow. For teachers, the conditions of employment and school standards often suffice—not to mention the average workload, which often leaves little room for online exploration.

However, the creativity and ingenuity of students opens up a flood of potential issues to be addressed. Most schools require that a student, and usually that student's parent or legal guardian, also sign the school's Acceptable Use Policy (*AUP*), in order to allow access to the school's online resources. Comprised of various regulations and conditions, the AUP is intended to protect the student and the school from the variety of problems that can occur in the day-to-day use of the Net.

Composing an AUP can often be a daunting task. In some cases, there may be only one or two people available at a school or in an entire school district with the experience and understanding to draft such a policy. Coupled with the legal issues regarding users' rights and the liability of the school, the hurdles of actually setting up computers and software can pale in comparison.

However, by consulting the existing AUPs of other schools and finding the common language included in them, actually creating the AUP becomes much less intimidating. Most importantly, the policy should be reviewed by the school's legal staff, or that of its district. While in an ideal setting the validity of the text included in the AUP will never be called into question, the reality is that schools must be confident that the document being signed will hold up in a legal court setting, should the need arise.

## Introductory Contents

Most AUPs begin with a description of the goals intended to be met by providing faculty and students with access to the Internet. Ranging from research for homework to email to live correspondence with other people across the globe, the Net opens up new horizons for learning. The breadth of the Internet itself is also usually pointed out, explaining that the school cannot maintain total control over what the users may run across.

Rather, those who sign such agreements are committing to abide by the rules and standards of behavior that are stated, as well as those of "common sense." When reading the policy, students are encouraged to review each part with their parents, asking questions about anything they may not understand. Unfortunately, children are not always open to this possibility—the phase of rebellion in the growing-up process can lead many to try to avoid interacting with their parents except when it's absolutely necessary. Thus, students have to understand that they are expected to comply with the agreement in order to keep their access to Cyberspace.

Having a child agree with rules they don't understand circumvents one of the primary goals of having such a policy: making people actively aware of what is considered improper behavior, or qualifies as being outside the scope of the original objective in offering use of the Internet.

Included in the initial paragraphs of AUPs is some text explaining the steps that will be taken in the event of a violation of the stated rules. Common results range from temporary suspension of access or forfeiture of the user's account, to legal action and expulsion. These actions are usually modeled after the same policies that are already present as general practice for the school in similar situations. Just as the sale of drugs on school grounds is against the rules and leads to strong penalties, activity online that is deemed illegal or unacceptable is met with similar consequences. However, most AUPs will explain the appropriate "due process," when used, that will be applied in the investigation and final decision regarding the breaking of a rule.

The complexity of the Internet requires that schools make sure their AUPs allow for future assessment of possible violations. The staff of a school needs the ability to decide whether or not a particular activity or use of their resources is considered as being against school policy. It should be clearly stated what person or group of people will decide what is and is not appropriate use as each issue comes up. This often involves the system administrator, a group of teachers, and sometimes representatives of the school district and the superintendent's office.

With the growth of the Net and its underlying technology, the crafting of an AUP cannot be expected to anticipate what users may encounter at some point down the road. The rules should allow for adaptation as the context of presence on the Internet continues to shift.

While not absolutely necessary, some AUPs also include information about proper Net etiquette, or "netiquette." This can involve checking your spelling, not typing all in upper case, and being polite.

To guard against user complaints, many schools remind people early in the policy that the staff and representatives of the school are not responsible for the validity or accuracy of information that may be found on the Internet. The statement that there is "no warrantee expressed or implied" protects the school against claims that they provided misleading or false information. Users are told that what they may find on the Internet should be used at their own risk— there are no standards applied to what people may make available to the Net community.

## Frequent Rules

The bulk of Acceptable Use Policies is the statement, and often the explanation, of the rules that must be followed. The possible choices for these rules is seemingly endless. There are a number of common items that are included in many of the existing AUPs being used today. In reading the policies of other schools, you may discover that a number of them are actually copies of other AUPs, often word for word. As one of the more frequent rules included points out, you should ask the permission of the original author before you make use of their work and ensure that you give them due credit. (For example, if much of your own policy is based on that of a particular school, mention that fact somewhere in the document.)

*School Responsibility*

The consistent reliability and "up time" of your system should not be assumed—explicitly stating that your school is not responsible for the inability to access a particular service on the Internet, or sporadic interruptions in attempts to transmit information, are beyond the control of most network sites, including schools. The attempt will be made to give a best effort at maintaining usability, but it should not be an absolute rule on the part of the people who work to keep the systems running.

*Harming Systems*

Among other things, vandalism of the school's equipment and resources is expressly forbidden. Similarly, tampering with the hardware and software of the equipment—playing with cords, switches, modifying installed software, et al.—can cause harm to the activity of other users. Deliberate disruption of the systems (running programs that effect others), or causing the network to be unusable for other people, can only make the overall system less usable.

*Software*

The introduction of viruses into the system, whether with a custom software package or a standard one used by many, should be specifically addressed. The actual installation of software on the system by students, or in some cases faculty, is forbidden, in order to avoid the presence of software viruses or the breaking of software license agreements. For example, the popularity of software piracy among some people could open the school up to legal action, since the software would be available to other users on the system. Thus, the involvement in software piracy of any form should be noted—coordinating the exchange of such files, knowingly downloading or uploading them, or telling others about their availability.

A few schools also include some language about the staff of the school only being allowed to develop software during school time if it's to be redistributed in the public domain and, specifically, not sold for commercial gain.

*Network Bandwidth*

The downloading of large files can cause the bandwidth of the school's network connection to be abated. As usually applies to software use, the playing of online games (e.g., multi-user dungeons, or *MUDs*) can have a similar negative effect to the general usability of the network.

*Use of Facilities*

The location of a school's computers often varies—for some, an entire lab is set up for access. Others have a single computer for a few, if not all, classrooms for use by each teacher. The resources available depend upon the interest of the local community, the funding available, and the physical structure of the school and its surroundings. The placement of the computers is often deliberate; schools will try to place the screens so that a person can stand at a particular point in the room and see what everyone is doing. Some schools take the extra step of saying that users are only allowed to use their equipment while under supervision, whether direct or simply having a staff member in the room.

An AUP can remind students of basic rules for the use of the facilities, including:

- Do not put anything on public hard disks—use floppy disks.
- Do not use waste or take supplies, like printer paper or disks.
- In some schools, users are required to sign in on a piece of paper before they can use the computers.
- Users must log off the computer when asked by a faculty member or the system administrator.
- People should talk softly and make sure their work doesn't disturb other users. (For example, if games are allowed, the sound usually should be turned off.)
- Users should log off when leaving for lunch or to go to a class.
- In many places, users are told that they have to log into the computer with a planned set of tasks to be done, so they don't squander time on the system while others are waiting for their turn.

The creation of a school environment for online discovery is a black art. When considering your own, you are encouraged to visit other schools and ask about their reasons for their choices of program, and what problems they may have run into since its inception.

*Illegal Activity*      The rules that apply to students as a part of the school's standard policy are also presented in most policies. They include:

- prohibiting the sale or exchange of drugs, or arranging the same
- advertising, selling, or purchasing illegal items of any kind
- transferring or obtaining sexually explicit material over the network
- engaging in computer stalking, in which the user actively sends harassing messages or threatens people in any manner

When reviewing the rules for illegal activity, it should be remembered that much of what can be done in real life can often be committed on the Internet. Any information or materials that are in direct violation of certain laws, whether local, state, or national in scope, usually qualify as such regardless of their setting. Students need to know that what is illegal in the "real" world is also illegal when done online.

*Plagiarism and Copyright Violations*      The information available on the Internet is owned by its creators; the copying of such information, or claiming that the words are your own, is a violation of the rules. The practice of plagiarism—basing your own creation on someone else's work without giving them due credit—is against the ethics of the educational profession and is not acceptable in any setting. Students need to know how to properly attribute a sentence, paragraph, or set of ideas for their own work based on its original source. There usually has to be a stated penalty for knowingly violating such a placement of copyright, whether specifically given or implied.

*Commercial/ Political Use*

The use of the resources for commercial or financial gain is not acceptable in a school environment. This can include advertising on the Net, whether via email, in a Usenet posting, or on a Web page.

Activity regarding political interests or lobbying is not allowed; this often takes the form of sending mail out to a number of people arguing the support of a particular candidate or ballot up for voter selection. Many schools also forbid lobbying related to the student body or student government, unless part of the system was specifically set up for such an activity.

*Electronic Mail*

The exchange of email messages, one of the most popular uses of the Internet, is itself open to a number of complications. In order to protect the school's administration from certain scenarios, AUPs usually cite a number of actions that are judged unacceptable.

 The forging of electronic mail so that it appears to have come from someone else.

Sending "anonymous" messages, in an attempt to hide not only the original user, but also the site that it came from.

 Most AUPs will mention that email is, in general, not a private form of communication. The actual text of a message can be seen by those who seek to "peek in" on such traffic. Similarly, the security of the recipient's system is not known to the sender— files may be openly readable by anyone on that computer.

 The redistribution of personal email from someone without that person's permission is not only rude, it's usually noted as a violation in the AUP.

 At some schools, you have to tell the system administrator (also termed the "lab operator") when you join a mailing list, and commit to regularly reading your messages. Otherwise, a mailbox can grow at an alarming rate, reducing the amount of disk space that's available to others.

 As can happen with postal mail, the exchange of electronic "chain letters" involves messages that say you must redistribute a particular note, usually to a certain number of people, in order to avoid impending bad luck or to receive your due fortune. While not easily enforced, prohibiting the redistribution of such chain letters, or at least requiring users to report that they were received to the appropriate teacher or system administrator, can help stem their continued circulation.

 Some sites require that users not use the system for sending or receiving a large number of personal messages, due to limitations regarding network speed or system space.

**Public Messages**

When people post a message to a Usenet newsgroup, or create a Web page, their email or Web address is sometimes interpreted as also representing

**Doonesbury**

BY GARRY TRUDEAU

their sponsoring site. The same can apply to email messages sent to a particular mailing list. When employees of a particular company create a home page, the fact that it's on a machine belonging to that company may lead some to believe that the employer knows about, and endorses, the contents of that page.

In fact, the actual contents of an individual's public post, message, or Web page is just that—an individual statement, and not the collective opinion or action of the containing organization. When an employee of a popular computer vendor sends an inflammatory message to a mailing list, most people realize that the voice of that one person is not backed up by the voice of the computer company. Likewise, a student or teacher is not representing their school when they craft a message or create a Web page.

In order to ensure that there is no possible misinterpretation of this fact, most schools require that people place a disclaimer at the end of any public email messages or newsgroup posts they make. A person's Web page will often include the same text somewhere, in order to make sure the reader knows that it's that person's own opinion, and theirs alone.

Along the same lines, to send messages that are in direct conflict with the code of conduct at that school is not allowed. Applying the same rule to messages received is more difficult—it must be qualified as messages that are actively received by the person. However, this rule covers, among other things, the possibility of a user sending a message to a newsgroup that flies in the face of school standards. Forbidding the use of inappropriate language falls under the same criteria, but is usually included as a separate rule.

Other common rules regarding public exchange include:

- Users are not allowed to take part in online flaming of another user, whether locally or in a more public forum.
- Publicly defaming people—posting or distributing messages in the form of libel or slander about a person with the goal of harming their reputation— is forbidden.
- Encouraging others to defame people in any way.
- Sending any messages conveying racism or bigotry is prohibited.
- Some schools specifically state that people should not imply or infer any form of gang affiliation.
- While many schools prohibit the exchange of online pictures of users, some allow it only when there is nothing on the picture identifying the person. (For example, a few allow them with initials included, but the majority of schools don't allow any such information to be transmitted.) Others extend the rule to apply to all forms of personal representation, including electronic movies and sound files.

*User and
System
Security*

As noted in the Safety chapter, users must know not to give out any form of personal information— their address, phone number, when they're at school or in a specific place. Most AUPs need to include this as part of the agreement, so students are reminded of these fundamental requirements.

It's often useful to mention in the agreement that children should tell someone when they find something that makes them feel at all uncomfortable, or discover something that they know probably isn't good to see. Their own judgment as far as what is "okay" often proves to be an excellent addition to the various rules they need to follow.

Some AUPs will include some discussion on how you can't tell the details about someone from what you see online. Their age, sex, whether or not they're telling the truth, all of these facts should only be believed with marginal trust when first "meeting" someone online.

If a student needs to give an address to someone online, they should check with their teacher or supervisor. If it's considered safe and allowable, the student should give the person on the other end the address of the school; they *absolutely should not* give their own home address. Also, the student should be reminded not to include their last name in such information. The better approach is for the student to ask for the other person's phone number, so the teacher can talk with them—partly because of their own interest in what's going to be sent, but also to verify the person's intentions. If the motives are not good, often the request for such a phone number will bring the offer to a sudden and dramatic halt. (This sort of occurrence should be reported to the system administrator of the school.)

The accounts (user IDs) and passwords used by people on a school's system are their most important concern. It's all too easy to have a person's identity adopted by someone else, not just in the form of forged email, but also in the form of messages or activity actually from their own account.

Regarding the user's own password, AUPs can include advice on how to pick one that's appropriate and secure: avoiding easily guessed words, using their own name, or their account's name itself. The frequent changing of the password is a good practice; while it can sometimes be difficult to remember which password you've chosen, using variations and easily remembered combinations of characters and numbers can help. Regardless of the choice of password, the practice of changing it periodically can dramatically reduce the ability of others to guess what it might be.

The use of someone else's account, even with permission, is usually forbidden. There should be no reason why a person's own account cannot be used—minor problems like forgotten passwords or system problems can be solved in short order. To try to break into someone else's account, or use their account, usually leads to that person's access being revoked. Likewise, the attempt to change that person's account, thus making it impossible for them to use it, is not acceptable.

An extreme of this situation, trying to use the account of the system administrator or person maintaining the system, can result not only in the blocking of access, but also some form of disciplinary action. The "power" of those accounts is what makes them more threatening; they often allow people to read any file on the system, or modify the computer in some fundamentally destructive way.

A user's files are their own; thus, people should not try to read or modify the files of others unless they are specifically given permission. Trying to copy another student's research paper online is just as inappropriate as photocopying it.

Some schools include restrictions based upon a particular person's history. If they are known to have caused problems on other computer systems, the proactive decision to block that person for any access can have some positive result. Be careful when applying this rule, though, since it's open to protest by both the student and his or her parents. The ability to make wise judgment in such cases is a difficult job.

If a user finds a security problem of any form, or knows of a particular misuse of the system (e.g., playing games or sending/receiving illegal information), they are encouraged to report it immediately to the system administrator. In particular, such discoveries of security problems should not be displayed or taught to other users.

*System Privacy*

The privacy of activity on a school network is open to interpretation. For some, the AUP will include the condition that the school preserves the right to monitor any and all traffic on the network at any time. This is occasionally reduced to say that the files and email of a user can be searched when necessary. Other variations include the system administrator having the right to view files on the system when trying to correct problems, or the user being notified when their files need to be accessed for whatever reason. Each school has to make their own decision about how much privacy their users will have, versus what is required in order to maintain the safety and operation of the network.

*Remote Systems*

The Internet makes it possible for people to make full use of the resources of other systems and networks. Those sites do not, however, let people take a free hand with their offerings. AUPs can specify that users must adhere to the rules of any remote systems they happen to use; if a particular Web site asks that users keep their activity to a minimum during a certain time period, remote users are expected to be courteous and heed the request. The attempt to break into remote systems is explicitly forbidden and could open the user up to legal action by the site being attacked.

## Qualifiers for Agreement

Aside from the various rules that are spelled out in an Acceptable Use Policy, most schools also require some qualifying steps before the student is allowed access. When possible, a student class or orientation is used to teach the students the basic use of the system, integrating the rules into the presentation so they're considered part of the proper handling of a person's access. Schools can take alternate approaches to the same goal, using a prepared video or a basic Internet test to make sure that the student understands the system and its proper use.

Parents are often just as interested, if not more, as their children about the school's use of the Internet. The frequent feeling of intimidation on the part of adults—their children knowing more about computers than they do—can be defeated by letting the parents learn along with their children. Evening sessions, similar to PTA meetings or parent-teacher conferences, can be used to teach parents about what the school has set up and answer their questions regarding their child's use of it. This can help parents view the AUP with their child later, knowing the issues to address and making sure their kids understand the document before signing it.

Variations on the basic theme behind agreement to the AUP can include:

- Having the student also include their student ID with their signature.
- Noting that the student's supervisor is also responsible for what occurs; this is a dangerous clause to include, unless reviewed and approved as necessary by the school's legal counsel.
- Some AUPs say that the sponsoring teacher will instruct the student about acceptable use and Net etiquette. Only include this when your teachers have time allocated to perform this task.

Again, the agreement that's being signed is open to legal interpretation. Having a legal representative endorse the language in the agreement is usually necessary to ensure that the signatures represent legal binding to the policy.

## Existing AUPs

There are a number of Web pages online offering collections of various AUPs from other schools. Many pages are also set up at each specific school, showing the agreement that they use for student access. They include:

1. Search for the term 'acceptable use policy' on any of the existing Internet search engines (including Yahoo and AltaVista[1]), and you will receive a number of links to various sites that have made their AUPs available.

2. A frequently asked questions (FAQ) list has been created to try to answer some of the more common questions that come up while drafting an AUP. Readers are encouraged to get a copy of this to help with the creation of their school or district's policy. To receive a copy, send an email message to the address

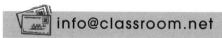
info@classroom.net

with the single line

    send aup-faq

in the body of the message. Alternatively, you can direct a Web browser at the URL

1. **Yahoo is at** http://www.yahoo.com/ **and AltaVista is at** http://www.altavista.digital.com/.

ftp://ftp.classroom.net/wentworth/Classroom-Connect/aup-faq.txt

to download a copy.

 You will find a variety of templates for AUPs at the URL

 http://www.erehwon.com/k12aup/

In addition, there is an excellent legal analysis of common language used by Nancy Willard, an Information Technology consultant with Internet Marketing Services. All of the contents of this collection are considered "honortext"—if you decide to use one of its templates, you are encouraged to send them a modest fee to support development of materials and learning activities addressing student ethical use of the Internet.

 As part of the AskERIC service, a compendium of AUPs is available via their gopher server. Point your Web browser at the URL

 gopher://ericir.syr.edu/11/Guides/Agreements

The collection isn't particularly extensive, but does give some excellent examples of real life policies.

 The Global SchoolNet Foundation has a collection of AUPs, along with guidelines for policy development; point your Web browser at the URL

 http://www.gsn.org/web/issues/aup/home.html

## AUP Mailing List

Finally, you can join a mailing list to seek help with creating your own policy. Among other benefits, the members of the list can point out issues or rules that they found were necessary.

To subscribe, send mail to the address

 k12-aup-request@merit.edu

with the single line

subscribe

in the body of the message. To leave the list, write to the same address with the body containing the line

unsubscribe

Messages intended for the whole list should be sent to the email address

 k12-aup@merit.edu.

*" "... suit the action to the word, the word to the action ..."*
— *Shakespeare*, Hamlet, Act 3 Scene 2

# Applying for Grants

**W**hile a lot of schools are getting funding right now for innovative work on using technology for K-12 education, the number of classrooms going online in the next year or two is going to make the competition fierce. That means it's becoming more and more important for educators to know how to write the kinds of grants that get funded.

Virginia Davis of Bryant Elementary School advises having strong goals, visions, and mission statements. You must be able to show how you've successfully integrated what resources you already have into your curriculum and how you plan to integrate what you're asking for. She suggests that every school write one background document with this information and then draw off of it when writing grants, using it as a common reservoir for all teachers.

For the purposes of writing grant proposals, the school's document must have two well-defined components in particular: support for student learning and plans for staff training.

Support for student learning is the heart of your grant applications. With the inundation of grant applications these organizations receive, they almost universally reject applications for hardware that do not include specific plans for integrating it into the school curriculum. Always keep in mind that technology is not the issue, education is.

Also, planning for staff training has become essential. Because funding is limited, a strong application shows how the school plans to make the most of the opportunity by training their teachers and passing on the results of their project to other educators. With limited resources, sharing is at an all-time premium.

It's always a good idea to research the organization you're applying to. Find their Web site and read up on what projects they've funded in the past. Remember that all of them are looking for new and undiscovered uses for technology in the classroom, and that most of them do not fund the same project more than once.

Although the organizations listed here are responsible for a lot of the funding in K-12 educational technology, these don't include the plethora of smaller grant foundations and corporations that offer funding you may be eligible for. The U.S. Department of Education has an extensive list of information on grants at their Web site at the URL

 http://www.ed.gov/

## U.S. Department of Education

The U.S. Department of Education operates two Programs of special interest to K-12 educators: OESE, the Office of Elementary and Secondary Education programs; and OERI, the Office of Educational Research & Improvement.

ESEA, the Elementary and Secondary Education Act of 1965, is the basis for OESE. Under OESE, ESEA has provisions for funding to a variety of educational technology areas. Also, the Goals 2000 Programs are intended to improve the use of technology in education.

One technological goal of the ESEA is providing educational technology to speed up the pace of school reform. Part A of Title III represents the department's and federal government's commitment to promote the use of technology in education.

Another goal is implementing the Innovative Education Strategies program. Title VI of ESEA supports a variety of local activities, including technology related to educational reform and funding for computer software and hardware.

And a third major technological goal is creating a new systemic approach to technical assistance for education. In looking for a new angle on the whole issue, Title XIII of ESEA provides for, among other services, technical assistance based on technology itself.

OERI was reauthorized as part of the GOALS 2000: Educate America Act. Research & Development—which includes most cutting edge educational technology—is meant to comprise at least one third of the grant awards.

Under OERI, the Center for Technology in Education administers a Field-Initiated Studies Program specifically aimed at research projects that use technology to improve education. This program is different from others in that the proposed project doesn't have to be part of any current focused research, so long as the results will have a significant impact on educational technology, which other educators can then build on.

Also under OERI, the Star Schools Program of the Office of Reform Assistance and Dissemination provides relevant grants. These grants are for eligible telecommunications partnerships covering most K-12 subject material. In addition, certain grants are available for local and statewide networking projects.

These are actually just a smattering of the grant opportunities available from the Department of Education. In particular, TLC, the Technology Learning Challenge, is worth looking up on the Web. Also, if you can prove that your project applies to one of the many other programs not listed here, which may not be specifically slated for educational technology, you may be eligible for funding through that one, also.

The OERI Information Office can be reached at (800) 424-1626 in the United States and Canada, or at (202) 219-1513 worldwide.

Contact the Center for Technology in Education at:

OERI Center for Technology in Education
Bank Street College of Education
610 West 112th Street
New York, NY 10025  USA
(212) 875-4200

Gregory Dennis, of the OERI Star Schools Program, can be reached at (202) 219-1919, or you can write to him in care of the Department of Education at the address listed below.

For Financial Aid information, call (800) 433-3243.

Through IRC, the Information Resource Center,[1] you can get information on anything within the Department of Education. They can be reached at:

 U.S. Department of Education
Information Resource Center
55 New Jersey Avenue NW
Washington, DC 20208-5530 USA
(800) USA-LEARN in the United States and Canada

## Networking Infrastructure for Education

NIE is a three-year program that began in 1994 under the auspices of the National Science Foundation (NSF), awarding grants for telecommunications programs in schools.

NIE's goal is to help develop a widespread infrastructure supporting electronic communications, specifically in education. NIE provides funding for a whole spectrum of educational fields—including science, math, engineering, and technology.

Like funding from the Department of Education, NIE funding is intended to lay the groundwork for further technological advances in education. EHR

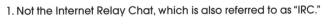

1. Not the Internet Relay Chat, which is also referred to as "IRC."

Assistant Director Dr. Luther Williams is very involved in educational reform and heavily emphasizes using technology to improve students' experiences in school.

Approved NIE projects look at policy issues that address technology in the classroom, networking at local and state levels and, in particular, educational planning. In fact, some planning grants have been so successful that the communities were able to take over financing their project and needed no further federal aid.

NIE application reviewers especially encourage K-12 educators to collaborate with university and community experts. They want to get the community thinking about innovative applications of technology that are strongly grounded in the classroom. They recommend concentrating on how technology impacts the educational and community infrastructure (the way things are handled by the school and the community) and on proactive dissemination of information, e.g. "getting the word out on the wonderful work being done by classroom teachers." NIE has tried to engage quality experts in higher education and K-12 to talk about how schools can develop access to technology.

Steven Sanchez of NIE recommends that educators visit the NIE Web site to research what types of projects the NIE has already funded and then use the results of that work to create new projects, building them into your own five-year curriculum plan. Be aware that the NSF does not fund the same project twice. Because it is a research institution, grants go to cutting edge exploratory projects, including testbeds for new technology and new approaches to education that use technology. Sanchez strongly suggests that you study the guidelines carefully in order to know what is and is not allowed, as applications for undeveloped projects—such as simply for hardware—are not approved.

Previous grant winners include Ed Friedman of NIE New Jersey, who developed training videos for teachers that became popular community broadcasts on PBS in New Jersey and New York; Jim Laffey of the University of Missouri, who received a one-year planning grant to develop computational science models, which were so successful that the grant was followed by a three-year grant to involve pre-service teachers in mentoring high school students; Kam Matray of the Monterey Unified School District, who created electronic field trips; and Eugene Klotz of Swarthmore, who has a large presence on the Web with his Mathematics Web page.

NIE is a joint effort between Directorates for Computer & Information Science & Engineering (CISE) and for Education & Human Resources (EHR). When the NIE program expires at the end of this fiscal year, the work that's been started is slated to be extended to all divisions of the EHR. Sanchez explains that technology is not the answer to problems in education, technology just helps move the solutions along.

Visit the NIE Web site for guidelines for grant proposals at:

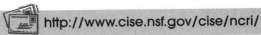
http://www.cise.nsf.gov/cise/ncri/

For further information, contact the NIE at:

National Science Foundation
Networking Infrastructure for Education
4201 Wilson Boulevard, Suite 855
Arlington, VA 22230 USA
nie@nsf.gov
(703) 306-1651

## National Telecommunications and Information Administration

NTIA operates under the direction of the U.S. Department of Commerce, funding educational technology through TIIAP, the Telecommunications & Information Infrastructure Assistance Program. TIIAP originated with NII when NII was passed by Congress in the fall of 1993.

In 1995, TIIAP received over 1,800 grant applications, requesting $680 million in federal funding and pledging more than $1.1 billion in matching funds. The greatest percent of those from one area came from the K-12 community, which accounted for almost a quarter of all grant applications (most other applications came from health care, economic development, library services, higher education, and public and government information).

However, NTIA and TIIAP funding was seriously threatened last September when HR 2076 was proposed to the Senate with major cuts to appropriations for Commerce, Justice and State, the Judiciary and related agendas, which includes NTIA. As of early

1996, there is still no budget for the Department of Commerce, but the federal bill under consideration has $21.5 million allocated for the TIIAP program.

According to Steve Downs, the Acting Director of TIIAP, there is a tremendous amount of potential in the K-12 community. He feels that the important thing for educators to do is to look at the projects TIIAP has already funded and contact the people who did them, to find out what other educators have learned. Like everyone else, TIIAP is looking for projects that demonstrate innovative uses for the NII.

For information about applications procedures and past grant winners, visit the TIIAP Web site at:

 http://www.ntia.doc.gov/tiiap/

For more information, contact Thomas Hardy at the address

 thardy@ntia.doc.gov

or write to:

 National Telecommunications & Information Administration
TIIAP
14th & Constitution Avenues NW, Room 4090
Washington, DC 20230 USA
(202) 482-2048
(202) 501-5136 Fax

## Cisco Education Program

Cisco Systems Inc. funds the 50 annual Cisco Internetworking Grants for educational institutions. In 1995, they received over 1,000 grant applications, and the winners were announced at the National Educational Computing Conference in June.

Cisco Systems Inc. was founded in 1984 at Stanford University, California, to produce internetworking products, and the Cisco Education Program was later established for the benefit of schools, museums, and libraries.

For information on grant application procedures and past grant winners, visit the URL

 http://sunsite.unc.edu/cisco/grant.html

To find out about applying for grants, contact the program at:

 Cisco Internetworking Grants
P.O. Box 14987
Research Triangle Park, NC 27709 USA
edu-grant@cisco.com
(800) EDNTWKS in the United States

*"Civil society has the right and duty of superintending and influencing education, inasmuch as education bears upon the child's capacity to become a member of society."*
— *G. W. F. Hegel*

# Glossary

The Internet sports its own dialect of the English language. Newly coined terms, phrases, and symbols have taken on common definition among its users. Below are some of the more common uses that you will encounter, along with the explanation for a few acronyms that may be referenced by people.

:-)  This odd symbol is one of the ways a person can portray "mood" in the very flat medium of computers—by using "smilies." This is "meta-communication," and there are literally hundreds of them, from the obvious to the obscure. This particular example expresses "happiness." Don't see it? Tilt your head to the left 90 degrees. Smilies are also used to denote sarcasm. There are actually a few small booklets on smilies available in many bookstores.

*Acceptable Use Policy (AUP)*   The definition of what is considered valid use of a particular network connection.

*anonymous FTP*   Also known as "anon FTP;" a service provided to make files available to the general Internet community.

*backbone*   A high-speed connection within a network that connects shorter, usually slower circuits. Also used in reference to a system that acts as a "hub" for activity (although those are becoming much less prevalent now than they were ten years ago).

*bandwidth*   The capacity of a medium to transmit a signal. More informally, the mythical "size" of the Net, and its ability to carry the files and messages of those that use it. Some view certain kinds of traffic (to FTP hundreds of graphics images, for example) as a "waste of bandwidth" and look down upon them.

*bounce*   The return of a piece of mail because of an error in its delivery.

*btw*   An abbreviation for "by the way."

*browser*   A software package used to access the World Wide Web.

*CACI*   Children Accessing Controversial Information.

*chat*   An online talk session, often with more than one person.

*client*   The user of a network service; also used to describe a computer that relies upon another for some or all of its resources.

*CoSN*   Consortium for School Networking.

*CU-SeeMe* Video conferencing software allowing Internet users to share live video and audio, regardless of distance.

*Cyberspace* A term coined by William Gibson in his fantasy novel *Neuromancer* to describe the "world" of computers and the society that gathers around them.

*domain* A part of the naming hierarchy. Syntactically, a domain name consists of a sequence of names or other words separated by dots.

*ERIC* Educational Resources Information Center.

*email* The vernacular abbreviation for electronic mail.

*email address* The address by which a user is referred to. For example, Janis Joplin's address might be janis@porsche.friend.org.

*flame* Mail or a Usenet posting that is violently argumentative.

*flamefest* Massive flaming.

*FTP (File Transfer Protocol)* The Internet standard high-level protocol for transferring files from one computer to another.

*GENII* Group Exploring the National Information Infrastructure.

*GUI (Graphical User Interface)* The aspects of a windowing system that make it unique; for example, the Motif GUI has a 3D feel to its buttons and menus.

*GSH* Global Schoolhouse.

*GVS*   Global Village Schools.

*header*   The portion of a packet, preceding the actual data, containing source and destination addresses and error-checking fields. Also part of a message or news article.

*hits*   Matches found in a search; e.g., a Web search for "NASA" will return a long list of hits for your query.

*home page*   A personal Web page.

*hostname*   The name given to a machine. (See also FQDN.)

*hotlist*   A person's selection of their favorite Web pages.

*IITA*   Information Infrastructure and Technology Administration.

*image map*   A graphic image on a Web page; you can click your mouse on a particular part of it to choose the next link you wish to visit.

*IMHO (In My Humble Opinion)*   This usually accompanies a statement that may bring about personal offense or strong disagreement.

*internet*   A collection of computers linked together by one or more networking protocols. An "internet" is not the same as "the Internet."

*the Internet*   A concatenation of many individual TCP/IP campus, state, regional, and national networks (such as NSFnet, AARNet, and Milnet) into one single logical network all sharing a common addressing scheme.

*Internet number*  The dotted-quad address used to specify a certain system. The Internet number for cs.widener.edu is 147.31.254.130. A resolver is used to translate between hostnames and Internet addresses.

*IRC*   Internet Relay Chat

*ISDN*   Integrated Services Digital Network. A fast, multi-channel connection for simultaneous high speed data and voice transmission.

*Internet Service Provider (ISP)*   A company or organization that provides connectivity to the Internet, whether through dedicated lines or dialup links.

*IP*   Internet Protocol

*ISTE*   International Society for Technology in Education.

*LAN (Local Area Network)*   Any physical network technology that operates at high speed over short distances (up to a few thousand meters).

*mail gateway*   A machine that connects to two or more electronic mail systems (especially dissimilar mail systems on two different networks) and transfers mail messages among them.

*mailing list*   A possibly moderated discussion group, distributed via email from a central computer, maintaining the list of people involved in the discussion.

*mail path*   A series of machine names used to direct electronic mail from one user to another.

*NCSA*   National Center for Supercomputing Applications.

*net.citizen* An inhabitant of Cyberspace. One usually tries to be a good net.citizen, lest one be flamed.

*netiquette* A pun on "etiquette;" proper behavior on the Net.

*network* A group of machines connected together so they can transmit information to one another. There are two kinds of networks: local networks and remote networks.

*newsgroup* A collection of messages on a particular topic, distributed via Usenet news.

*nickname* The name attached to a message displayed in IRC.

*NSF* National Science Foundation.

*NII* National Information Infrastructure.

*packet* The unit of data sent across a packet switching network. The term is used loosely.

*postmaster* The person responsible for taking care of mail problems, answering queries about users, and performing similar work for a given site.

*route* The path that network traffic takes from its source to its destination.

*router* A dedicated computer (or other device) that sends packets from one place to another, paying attention to the current state of the network.

*RTFM (Read The Fantastic Manual)* This acronym is often used when someone asks a simple or common question. The word "Fantastic" is usually replaced with one much more vulgar.

*server*   A computer that shares its resources, such as printers and files, with other computers on the network. Also known for its service—e.g., a *Web server* provides access to a set of Web pages.

*signature*   The small, usually four-line message at the bottom of a piece of email or Usenet article. Large signatures are a no-no.

*smilies*   See :-).

*spam*   Blatant and high-volume Internet advertising, often performed by sending mail to hundreds of mailing lists simultaneously, or by posting an advertisement to thousands of newsgroups. The most aggressive approach to performing a *spam attack* is to meticulously make the posting to each group separately, thus making cancellation of the article difficult and time-consuming.

*TCP/IP   (Transmission   Control   Protocol/Internet Protocol)*   A set of protocols, resulting from ARPA efforts, used by the Internet to support services such as remote login (telnet), file transfer (FTP), and mail (SMTP).

*telnet*   The Internet standard protocol for remote terminal connection service. Telnet allows a user at one site to interact with a remote timesharing system at another site as if the user's terminal were connected directly to the remote computer.

*TIA*   Thanks In Advance. Also, those who are very clever sometimes use the interesting form aTdH-vAaNnKcSe.

*twisted pair*   Cable made up of a pair of insulated copper wires wrapped around each other to cancel the effects of electrical noise.

*URL* Uniform Resource Locator. The identifier for accessing a given World Wide Web page, FTP site, et al.

*Webmaster* Person given the task of setting up and maintaining a site's Web server and pages.

*WWW (World Wide Web)* The interface used to present graphics, information, tables, and forms in a user-friendly setting.

*wrt* With respect to.

*"A definition is the enclosing a wilderness of idea within a wall of words."*

— *Samuel Butler,* Notebooks

# Bibliography

**T**he number of books addressing children and the Internet are increasing at a remarkable rate; keep your eyes open for new approaches as they appear in bookstores. Included in this list are some of those books and related magazine and news articles, along with others that will be helpful as you explore Cyberspace with your kids.

## Books

**Baran, Nicholas** (1995). *Inside the Information Superhighway.* The Coriolis Group: Scottsdale, AZ.

**Cummins, Jim, and Dennis Sayers** (1995). *Brave New Schools: Challenging Cultural Illiteracy Through Global Learning Networks.* St. Martin's Press: New York, NY.

Dern, Daniel P. (1994). *The Internet Guide for New Users.* McGraw-Hill: New York, NY.

Ellsworth, J. H. (1994). *Education on the Internet: A Hands-on Book of Ideas, Resources, Projects, and Advice.* Sams Publishing: Indianapolis, IN.

Estrada, Susan (1993). *Connecting to the Internet.* O'Reilly and Associates: Sebastopol, CA.

Frazier, Deneen, with Barbara Kurshan and Sara Armstrong (1995). *Internet for Kids.* Sybex: Alameda, CA.

Giagnocavo, G., et. al. (1995). *Educator's Internet Companion.* Wentworth Worldwide Media: Lancaster, PA.

Gibbs, Mark, and Richard Smith (1995). *Navigating the Internet.* Sams Publishing: Carmel, IN.

Gilster, Paul (1994). *Finding It On the Internet.* John Wiley & Sons: New York, NY.

Hafner, Katie, and John Markoff (1991). *Cyberpunk: Outlaws and Hackers on the Computer Frontier.* Simon & Schuster: New York, NY.

Krol, Ed (1992). *The Whole Internet User's Guide and Catalog.* O'Reilly and Associates: Sebastopol, CA.

MKS Inc. (1995). *Internet Anywhere.* Prentice Hall: Englewood Cliffs, NJ.

Parker, Tracy LaQuey, and Jeanne C. Ryer (1994). *The Internet Companion: A Beginner's Guide to Global Networking.* Addison-Wesley: Reading, MA.

LaQuey, Tracy (1990). *Users' Directory of Computer Networks.* Digital Press: Bedford, MA.

Marine, April, et al. (1994). *Internet: Getting Started.* SRI International: Menlo Park, CA.

Pederson, Ted, and Francis Moss (1995). *Internet For Kids.* Price Stern Sloan: Los Angeles, CA.

Polly, Jean Armour (1996). *The Internet Kids Yellow Pages*. McGraw-Hill: Berkeley, CA.

Protheroe, N. and E. Wilson (1994). *The Internet Handbook for School Users*. Educational Research Service: Arlington, VA.

Rheingold, Howard (1993). *The Virtual Community*. Harper Perennial: New York, NY.

Rose, Donald (1994). *Minding Your Cyber-Manners on the Internet*. Alpha Books: Indianapolis, IN.

Ross, Calvin (1995). *Whiz Kid Starter Kit*. Patson's Press: Sunnyvale, CA.

Salzman, Marian and Pondiscio, Robert (1995). *Kids On-Line*. Avon Books: New York, NY.

Steen, D.R., M.R., Roddy, D., Sheffield, and M.B. Stout (1995). Teaching with the Internet: Putting Teachers Before Technology. Resolution Business Press: Bellevue, WA.

Stoll, Clifford (1995). *Silicon Snake Oil*. Doubleday: New York, NY.

Tamosaitis, Nancy (1994). *net.talk*. Ziff-Davis Press: Emeryville, CA.

Tennant, Roy, John Ober, and Anne G. Lipow, ed. (1993). *Crossing the Internet Threshold: An Instructional Handbook*. Library Solutions Press: Berkeley, CA.

Williams, Bard (1995). *The Internet for Teachers*. IDG Books: Foster City, CA.

## Periodicals and Papers

Alexander, S. "Curiosity key motivator in surfing the Internet." *Star Tribune* (March 6, 1995): 1D.

Andres, Y. "Education On-Line." *Executive Educator* (June 1993): 21-23.

Burleigh, M. and P. Weeg. "KIDLINK: a challenge and safe place for children across the world." *Information Development* (September 1993): 147-57.

Business Week. Special issue on the Information Revolution. (May 18, 1994).

Chock, P.N. "The use of computers in the sexual exploitation of children and child pornography." *Computer/Law Journal* (Summer 1987): 383-407.

Connell, T.H. and C. Franklin. "The Internet: educational issues." *Library Trends* (Spring 1994): 608-625.

Crawley, J. "Schools need Internet hookups, not TV." *San Diego Union-Tribune* (September 27, 1994): 6.

Cuban, L. "Computers Meet Classroom: Who Wins?" *Education Digest* (March 1994): 50-53.

de Llosa, P. "Boom Time on the New Frontier." *Fortune* (Autumn 1993): 153-164.

de Vries, P. J. L. and K. Auerbach. "Guide to Selecting an Internet Provider." *Network Computing* (May 15, 1995): 120.

Doty, R. "Teacher's Aid." *Internet World* (March 1995): 75-77.

____. "Curriculum Counselor." *Internet World* (October 1995): 76-79.

Dresang, J. "Policing Cyberspace." *Milwaukee Journal Sentinel* (December 10, 1995): 1.

Fitzpatrick, M. L. "The Global Classroom." *Chicago Tribune* (June 25, 1995): 3.

Franklin, C. Jr. "A Glossary of Internet Terms." *Var Business* (September 1, 1994): 70.

Halvonik, S. "Can the Internet be sanitized?" Pittsburgh Post-Gazette (July 25, 1995): C4.

Harris, J. "Mining the Internet: Using Internet Know-How to Plan How Students Will Know." *Computing Teacher* (May 1993): 35-40.

Hoye, D. "Take Safety Precautions When Traveling Internet." *Phoenix Gazette* (September 18, 1995): G1.

Kane, P. "The New LIBRARY." *NetGuide* (September 1995): 36-39.

Killian, C. "Why Teachers Fear the Internet." *Internet World* (November/December 1994): 86-87.

Larrabee, J. "Cyberspace a new beat for police." *USA Today* (April 26, 1994): 1A.

Lieberman, D. "Teens for Telnet, K-12 and the Internet. "*Internet World* (January/February 1994): 38-42.

Llanos, M. "Classroom Connections—Area schools take kids and teachers on electronic field trips." *Seattle Times* (January 15, 1995): C1.

Messmer, E. "Internet Retrieval Tools Go On Market." *Network World* (Feb. 15, 1993): 29.

Murray, J. "K12 network: global education through telecommunications." *Communications of the ACM* (August 1993): 36-41.

*NetGuide* Magazine, *For Kids Only* section.

Pearlman, R. "Restructuring with Technology: A Tour of Schools Where It's Happening." *Technology & Learning* (January 1991): 30-37.

Polly, J. A. *Surfing the INTERNET: an Introduction.* Excellent and entertaining guide to the Net. *Surfing* is available on nysernet.org in the directory 'pub/resources/guides'.

Radisich, B.J. "Networking your school: the pros and cons." *Media and Methods* (March-April 1994): 47-48.

Sanchez, R. A. "Wired Education." *Internet World* (October 1995): 71-74.

**Sanford, R.** "Internet's Reality, Potential Spreading; Morenet Puts Missouri 'Ahead Of Most States'." *St. Louis Post-Dispatch* (November 27, 1994): 1E.

**Shapiro, N., and R. Anderson.** *Toward an Ethics and Etiquette for Electronic Mail.* Santa Monica, CA: RAND Corporation, Report R-3283-NSF/RC. Available on rand.org in 'pub/Reports'.

**Smith, K.** "E-Mail to Anywhere." *PC World* (March 1988): Stanton, D. *AARNet and the Academic Library: A Report on the Seminar/Workshop Held February 1992.* Murdoch, W.A.: Murdoch University Library. Available via anonymous FTP from csuvax1.csu.murdoch.edu.au in 'pub/library' as 'newcwkshp.rpt'.

**Strangelove, M.** "At Play in the Fields of the Internet." *Online Access* (September 1993): 18-22.

**Taylor, D.** "The Best Education Resources." *Internet World* (January 1995): 40.

**Vacca, J. R.** "CU on the Net." *Internet World* (October 1995): 80-82.

**Williams, A.** "Internet: Giving a Voice To Those Without." *The Guardian* (May 25, 1995): 6.

**Wright, R.** "Voice of America: Overhearing the Internet." *The New Republic* (September 13, 1993): 20-27.

*"Books must follow sciences, and not sciences books."*
—*Francis Bacon*, Resuscitatio

# Index

# THE INTERNET

NOW RATED
## PG

**PARENTAL GUIDANCE. JUST WHAT CYBERSPACE HAS BEEN MISSING.**

   With just a click and a password, you can block all the objectionable Internet sites using Cyber Patrol's thoroughly researched (and regularly updated) CyberNOT list. Or, you can specify your own access preferences, in as much detail as you like. Try the CyberYES Allowed Sites List- its thousands of researched Internet sites contain only fun and educational material for children.

Cyber Patrol provides:
- Multi-user capability - allowing online access to be customized for each family member or group of students
- The ChatGard® feature which prevents children from divulging personal information online - such as name, phone number, e-mail address, etc.
- The first and only Internet filter that works with all browsers in use at home or school
- The ability to set ground rules for total time spent online, by total hours or by time of day

   Now they can explore... and you can relax.  More parents and educators trust Cyber Patrol than any other filtering software - you can too!

**Turn the page...**
**and choose the Cyber Patrol Special Offer that is right for you !**

Microsystems Software, Inc.   tel: 800-828-2608   e-mail: info@microsys.com   http://www.cyberpatrol.com

# Cyber Patrol Special Offers

## Cyber Patrol Home Edition

Cyber Patrol Home Edition - with basic Internet filtering - is now available for FREE!

You can download Cyber Patrol from the Internet at: http://www.cyberpatrol.com

## Home Users

Home Users -- Receive a 10% Discount on Cyber Patrol full version!
(Includes 3-month subscription to CyberNOT and CyberYES Lists.)

• **Online Respondents:**

To get your 10% discount, enter the code "CP-10" on the second address line (Addr2)
of the Online Registration Screen.
(Includes 3-month subscription to CyberNOT and CyberYES Lists.)

• **Telephone Respondents:**

To get your 10% discount, mention code "CP-10" when you place your order.
(Includes 3-month subscription to CyberNOT and CyberYES Lists.)

## Schools

Receive 1 Free Copy of Cyber Patrol for Every 10 Copies Purchased!
All 10 copies of Cyber Patrol must be purchased at one time to qualify.
(Includes 12-month subscription to CyberNOT and CyberYES Lists.)

Call Microsystems Cyber Patrol Educational Sales Department at 800-828-2608
and mention code "CP-10" to take advantage of this offer.

## Visit us online at http://www.cyberpatrol.com

Microsystems Software, Inc.   600 Worcester Road   Framingham  MA   01702
fax: 508-626-8515  e-mail: info@microsys.com ©1996 Microsystems Software Inc.

# CYBERsitter

---

## Ordering Information:

**Please send me CYBERsitter for only $29.95**

Name: _____

Company: _____

Address: _____

City: _____

State: _____ Zip: _____Phone: _____

Credit Card (MC, Visa, Amex)  No:_____ Exp:_____

**Please Complete and mail to:**
Solid Oak Software, Inc. - P.O. Box 6826 - Santa Barbara, CA
Or call: (805)967- 9853 - Fax (805)-892-2550

Don't Forget to Visit our Web Site at: www.solidoak.com

# dax*HOUND*

## *how it works*

Using Net Shepherd Inc.'s unique dax*HOUND* software, you - as the Net Shepherd Administrator - set up individual, password-protected accounts to allow rating privileges or restrict Internet access. When you're logged in as an Administrator, Net Shepherd's point-and-click ratings bar becomes part of your browser window, allowing you to rate page as you surf.

To rate a page, all you have to do is click on a rating button, and dax*HOUND* does the rest. The rating value is permanently stored in a dax*HOUND* database on your local hard drive. dax*HOUND* then automatically transmits your ratings to a central, on-line Net Shepherd database known as a 'Label Bureau'. The Label Bureau database automatically compiles the ratings it receives from you and other dax*HOUND* users in the Internet community to create a collaboratively rated value for each page. You can subscribe to any Label Bureau or Bureaus you choose, knowing that their databases reflect the collective opinions of their subscriber communities.

When a filtered user is logged in, dax*HOUND* restricts access based on the privileges you define when you set up the user account. When the user requests a page, dax*HOUND* checks for a rating value in its database on the local hard drive. If no rating is found, it requests a rating 'lookup' from a Net Shepherd Rating Label Bureau. In this way, the collaborative rating of all label bureau contributors is used only when you have not rated the page yourself. When Net Shepherd software finds a rating value that is inappropriate for the filtered user, access is denied. You can choose to deny access to all unrated pages.

dax*HOUND* - the **best** way to filter, the **only** way to rate!

*email* info@shepherd.net
*on the web* http://www.shepherd.net

## *The Internet Filter*

is an Internet Access Control Software package that will

- block
- log violations
- forward logged violations and
- restrict computer usage to "Good Sites" only

*It is comprehensive and complete.*

There are two versions. Both available for download at:

### http://www.turnercom.com

Version Zero blocks "bad sites" and is free. Version One is configurable and comprehensive; Version One is $40,00 US funds.

**The Internet Filter is for Windows 95 and 3.1**

Also available from
Bob Turner, Box 151 - 3456 Dunbar St., Vancouver BC Canada V6S 2C2
bturner@direct.ca — phone/fax 604-708-2397

It is produced by J.D. Koftinoff Software Ltd.
and Turner Investigations, Research and Communications

*Special offer from*

**SURF WATCH.** ™
*Protect your kids
on the Net.*

**SurfWatch** is a breakthrough software product that helps parents and educators deal with the flood of sexually explicit material on the Internet. SurfWatch allows users to limit unwanted material locallty without restricting the access rights of other Internet users.

**SurfWatch** screens Internet newsgroups, WWW, FTP, Gopher, Chat and other services.

## Key Features

- Screens for newsgroups likely to contain sexually explicit material
- Keeps your computer from accessing specified World Wide Web, FTP, Gopher, Chat and other sites
- Subscription automatically updates blocked site list
- Customized lists are available
- Fast and easy to install

## System Requirements

- Macintosh or Power Macintosh
- System 7.x with MacTCP 2.0 or higher
- Windows 3.1 enhanced on 386 PC/4MB RAM(486/8MEG highly recommended), Microsoft compatible, Winsock
- Direct access to the Internet via modem, ISDN, or high-speed link

Software suggested retail price is $49.95
*Special offer is for $19.95*
**Call 800-458-6600**
Must mention coupon

## LICENSE AGREEMENT AND LIMITED WARRANTY

READ THE FOLLOWING TERMS AND CONDITIONS CAREFULLY BEFORE OPENING THIS SOFTWARE PACKAGE. THIS LEGAL DOCUMENT IS AN AGREEMENT BETWEEN YOU AND PRENTICE-HALL, INC. (THE "COMPANY"). BY OPENING THIS SEALED CD PACKAGE, YOU ARE AGREEING TO BE BOUND BY THESE TERMS AND CONDITIONS. IF YOU DO NOT AGREE WITH THESE TERMS AND CONDITIONS, DO NOT OPEN THE CD PACKAGE. PROMPTLY RETURN THE UNOPENED CD PACKAGE AND ALL ACCOMPANYING ITEMS TO THE PLACE YOU OBTAINED THEM FOR A FULL REFUND OF ANY SUMS YOU HAVE PAID.

1.    **GRANT OF LICENSE:** In consideration of your purchase of this book, and your agreement to abide by the terms and conditions of this Agreement, the Company grants to you a nonexclusive right to use and display the copy of the enclosed software program (hereinafter the "SOFTWARE") on a single computer (i.e., with a single CPU) at a single location so long as you comply with the terms of this Agreement. The Company reserves all rights not expressly granted to you under this Agreement.

2.    **OWNERSHIP OF SOFTWARE:** You own only the magnetic or physical media (the enclosed CD) on which the SOFTWARE is recorded or fixed, but the Company and the software developers retain all the rights, title, and ownership to the SOFTWARE recorded on the original CD copy(ies) and all subsequent copies of the SOFTWARE, regardless of the form or media on which the original or other copies may exist. This license is not a sale of the original SOFTWARE or any copy to you.

3.    **COPY RESTRICTIONS:** This SOFTWARE and the accompanying printed materials and user manual (the "Documentation") are the subject of copyright. The individual programs on the CD are copyrighted by the authors of each program. Some of the programs on the CD include separate licensing agreements. If you intend to use one of these programs, you must read and follow its accompanying license agreement. You may <u>not</u> copy the Documentation or the SOFTWARE, except that you may make a single copy of the SOFTWARE for backup or archival purposes only. You may be held legally responsible for any copying or copyright infringement which is caused or encouraged by your failure to abide by the terms of this restriction.

4.    **USE RESTRICTIONS:** You may <u>not</u> network the SOFTWARE or otherwise use it on more than one computer or computer terminal at the same time. You may physically transfer the SOFTWARE from one computer to another provided that the SOFTWARE is used on only one computer at a time. You may <u>not</u> distribute copies of the SOFTWARE or Documentation to others. You may <u>not</u> reverse engineer, disassemble, decompile, modify, adapt, translate, or create derivative works based on the SOFTWARE or the Documentation without the prior written consent of the Company.

5.    **TRANSFER RESTRICTIONS:** The enclosed SOFTWARE is licensed only to you and may <u>not</u> be transferred to any one else without the prior written consent of the Company. Any unauthorized transfer of the SOFTWARE shall result in the immediate termination of this Agreement.

6.    **TERMINATION:** This license is effective until terminated. This license will terminate automatically without notice from the Company and become null and void if you fail to comply with any provisions or limitations of this license. Upon termination, you shall destroy the Documentation and all copies of the SOFTWARE. All provisions of this Agreement as to warranties, limitation of liability, remedies or damages, and our ownership rights shall survive termination.

7.    **MISCELLANEOUS:** This Agreement shall be construed in accordance with the laws of the United States of America and the State of New York and shall benefit the Company, its affiliates, and assignees.

8.    **LIMITED WARRANTY AND DISCLAIMER OF WARRANTY:** The Company warrants that the SOFTWARE, when properly used in accordance with the Documentation, will operate in substantial conformity with the description of the SOFTWARE set forth in the Documentation. The Company does not warrant that the SOFTWARE will meet your requirements or that the operation

of the SOFTWARE will be uninterrupted or error-free. The Company warrants that the media on which the SOFTWARE is delivered shall be free from defects in materials and workmanship under normal use for a period of thirty (30) days from the date of your purchase. Your only remedy and the Company's only obligation under these limited warranties is, at the Company's option, return of the warranted item for a refund of any amounts paid by you or replacement of the item. Any replacement of SOFTWARE or media under the warranties shall not extend the original warranty period. The limited warranty set forth above shall not apply to any SOFTWARE which the Company determines in good faith has been subject to misuse, neglect, improper installation, repair, alteration, or damage by you. EXCEPT FOR THE EXPRESSED WARRANTIES SET FORTH ABOVE, THE COMPANY DISCLAIMS ALL WARRANTIES, EXPRESS OR IMPLIED, INCLUDING WITHOUT LIMITATION, THE IMPLIED WARRANTIES OF MERCHANTABILITY AND FITNESS FOR A PARTICULAR PURPOSE. EXCEPT FOR THE EXPRESS WARRANTY SET FORTH ABOVE, THE COMPANY DOES NOT WARRANT, GUARANTEE, OR MAKE ANY REPRESENTATION REGARDING THE USE OR THE RESULTS OF THE USE OF THE SOFTWARE IN TERMS OF ITS CORRECTNESS, ACCURACY, RELIABILITY, CURRENTNESS, OR OTHERWISE.

IN NO EVENT, SHALL THE COMPANY OR ITS EMPLOYEES, AGENTS, SUPPLIERS, OR CONTRACTORS BE LIABLE FOR ANY INCIDENTAL, INDIRECT, SPECIAL, OR CONSEQUENTIAL DAMAGES ARISING OUT OF OR IN CONNECTION WITH THE LICENSE GRANTED UNDER THIS AGREEMENT, OR FOR LOSS OF USE, LOSS OF DATA, LOSS OF INCOME OR PROFIT, OR OTHER LOSSES, SUSTAINED AS A RESULT OF INJURY TO ANY PERSON, OR LOSS OF OR DAMAGE TO PROPERTY, OR CLAIMS OF THIRD PARTIES, EVEN IF THE COMPANY OR AN AUTHORIZED REPRESENTATIVE OF THE COMPANY HAS BEEN ADVISED OF THE POSSIBILITY OF SUCH DAMAGES. IN NO EVENT SHALL LIABILITY OF THE COMPANY FOR DAMAGES WITH RESPECT TO THE SOFTWARE EXCEED THE AMOUNTS ACTUALLY PAID BY YOU, IF ANY, FOR THE SOFTWARE.

SOME JURISDICTIONS DO NOT ALLOW THE LIMITATION OF IMPLIED WARRANTIES OR LIABILITY FOR INCIDENTAL, INDIRECT, SPECIAL, OR CONSEQUENTIAL DAMAGES, SO THE ABOVE LIMITATIONS MAY NOT ALWAYS APPLY. THE WARRANTIES IN THIS AGREEMENT GIVE YOU SPECIFIC LEGAL RIGHTS AND YOU MAY ALSO HAVE OTHER RIGHTS WHICH VARY IN ACCORDANCE WITH LOCAL LAW.

ACKNOWLEDGMENT

YOU ACKNOWLEDGE THAT YOU HAVE READ THIS AGREEMENT, UNDERSTAND IT, AND AGREE TO BE BOUND BY ITS TERMS AND CONDITIONS. YOU ALSO AGREE THAT THIS AGREEMENT IS THE COMPLETE AND EXCLUSIVE STATEMENT OF THE AGREEMENT BETWEEN YOU AND THE COMPANY AND SUPERSEDES ALL PROPOSALS OR PRIOR AGREEMENTS, ORAL, OR WRITTEN, AND ANY OTHER COMMUNICATIONS BETWEEN YOU AND THE COMPANY OR ANY REPRESENTATIVE OF THE COMPANY RELATING TO THE SUBJECT MATTER OF THIS AGREEMENT.

Should you have any questions concerning this Agreement or if you wish to contact the Company for any reason, please contact in writing at the address below.

Robin Short

Prentice Hall PTR

One Lake Street

Upper Saddle River, New Jersey 07458